REMEDIES
IN A
NUTSHELL

By

JOHN F. O'CONNELL
Professor of Law
Western State University College of Law

SECOND EDITION

ST. PAUL, MINN.
WEST PUBLISHING CO.
1985

COPYRIGHT © 1977 By WEST PUBLISHING CO.
COPYRIGHT © 1985 By WEST PUBLISHING CO.

610 Opperman Drive
P.O. Box 64526
St. Paul, MN 55164–0526
1–800–328–9352

All rights reserved
Printed in the United States of America

ISBN 0–314–85066–X

9th Reprint — 2003

TO ROSEMARY

The Mother of our Six Children
Four of Whom are Lawyers

*

III

PREFACE

This book, like its predecessor, is for the law student.

The subject of Remedies is one of the most difficult of all of the subjects in law school because of its comprehensiveness. Before one can even begin to undertake its study, he/she should have completed courses in Contracts, Torts, Real Property, Community Property, Civil Procedure, Constitutional Law and Corporations, just to name a few of the more important substantive courses. This is because of the general rule that the specific remedy follows the substantive course. In this respect, therefore, Remedies does serve as a review of the substantive law in those other courses; however, the emphasis should be placed on the remedy itself. Some law schools accomplish this by integrating the rules of Remedies into the substantive courses rather than by teaching Remedies as a separate subject. It is akin to integrating Agency and Partnership into Business Associations.

The original edition of this Nutshell has been used by students in law schools throughout the country for the past seven years. Approval has been expressed of the format, its conversational style, simplicity of explanation, feasibility for study, and applicability to examination problem solving. Suggested improvements, particularly in the organization of the material, have been incorporated in this new edition.

Despite the efforts made to reduce the volume of material to a manageable level, students are still faced with the problem of developing an approach for studying and mastering the material. Without such an approach, the forest is still a forest even though a smaller one. The following paragraphs, therefore, will attempt to provide that approach.

Despite the mass and volume of the material in Remedies, there are really only six major remedies to contend with: Injunction, Restitution, Compensatory Damages, Rescission, Reformation, and Specific Performance. The course in Remedies, whether designated as Remedies I and II, or Damages and Equity I and II, or simply as Remedies, splits rather evenly into those remedies both at law and in equity for torts and contracts. Looking at the major remedies, those of Injunction, Restitution, and Compensatory Damages apply to the torts because one does not rescind a tort, or reform a tort, and, certainly, one does not ask an equity court to specifically perform a tort. Remedies for the breach of a contract, however, may involve all six of the major remedies, e.g., you can get an Injunction to enforce a negative convenant in an employment contract; or, Restitution for unjust gains made by breaching an agreement; losses (Compensatory Damages) for the breach of the contract; you can get it rescinded, reformed, and specifically performed. Thus, as a starting point, the student should determine immediately if his fact pattern deals only with torts in which case he would consider the applicable remedies of Injunction, Restitution, and/or Compensatory Damages. If only contracts are involved or a combination of torts and contracts in the same fact pattern, the student would have to consider the application of all six of the major remedies.

Another approach to using the remedies, is to distinguish between those used in equity and those used at law. It will be noticed immediately that equity not only has the most remedies, but also the best remedies, e.g., Injunction, Reformation, and Specific Performance are peculiar to equity which also uses the remaining remedies of Restitution, Compensatory Damages and Rescission. At law, however, one can look only to Restitution, Compensatory Damages and Rescission.

Because the remedies in equity are superior to those at law, equity restricts the access to its court by requiring that the remedy at law must be inadequate. Case law provides several common reasons for such inadequacy, viz., land is unique, chattel is unique, breach of a fiduciary relationship, multiplicity of suits, damages are too speculative, or there is no remedy at law. Applying these bases for equity jurisdiction to torts and contracts, it can be readily seen that the one most commonly used for torts is that of multiplicity of suits, i.e., a tort of a continuing nature, followed by damages being too speculative. The others fit very nicely into breach of contract situations. With respect to "no remedy at law," one must refer to the Bill of Accounting and Reformation, neither of which are given at law.

Once in equity, the student will find that the most commonly used remedies are those of Injunction and Specific Performance. Both of these have certain elements which must be satisfied before they can be used. In the case of the Injunction, these elements usually are the Tort, Adequacy of the remedy at law, Enforceability, Property Right, Balancing of the Hardships, and Defenses (Laches or Unclean Hands). In that of Specific Performance, the elements are a valid Contract, Adequacy of the remedy at law, Enforceability, Mutuality of Performance, no outstanding Conditions, Defenses (Laches, Unclean Hands, or any defense to a contract such as the Statute of Frauds), Equitable Conversion (in land sales contracts only).

To assist the student in applying the above major approaches, this Nutshell has been divided into two major sections. Section "A" discusses the legal and equitable remedies which are available while Section "B" applies those remedies to specific fact situations. Section "B" has been further divided into the application of appropriate remedies for torts and those for the breach of contracts. Tying the above approaches to the material in this Nutshell, the student can use the following suggested schematic to handle any torts on a purely Remedies type of fact pattern: (1) Identify the tort; (2) Define it; (3) Use the facts from the problem to support the tort; (4) Discuss the applicable remedies of Injunction, Restitution, and/or Compensatory Damages.

For a breach of contract situation, the student may apply the following suggested schematic: (1) Determine the validity of the contract; (2) find its major condition; (3) see where this condition fails; (4) find the breach of the promise to do the same thing which is contained in the condition; (5) make sure the breach is material; (6) apply the appropriate remedies to the type of contract involved, i.e., Injunction (only to enforce a negative covenant in an employment contract), Restitution, Compensatory Damages, Rescission, Reformation, and Specific Performance.

It should be readily noticeable to the student that in a purely Remedies type of problem, the torts will be there and the contract will be breached; otherwise, one would never reach the remedies. In a cross-over question, however, one must be careful to insure that either the tort or the contract is valid before proceeding to a discussion of the remedies.

This new edition, therefore, not only provides a succinct exposition of the law of Remedies to which a student can turn for guidance but also is designed with one goal in mind, viz., student utility in this difficult area of the law. As one who instructs in this subject, I would advise the student to use this Nutshell as an adjunct to the leading hornbooks and casebooks on Remedies, although some of my own students have told me that they used only the Nutshell to prepare for the bar and had no difficulty in passing the Remedies portion thereof.

Jᴏʜɴ F. O'Cᴏɴɴᴇʟʟ

Fullerton, California

ACKNOWLEDGMENTS

I wish to acknowledge the painstaking efforts of Evie Rubin, a former student in my class and a graduate of Western State University College of Law, for her assistance in proofreading the drafts for this book.

I wish also to acknowledge the use of information from the scholarly article written by Attorney Joseph Zallen for Case and Comment (Vol. 80, #4) entitled "Product Protection for Inventors and Manufacturers." In addition, the following Restatement excerpts were reprinted with the permission of The American Law Institute:

Restatement of the Law, Second, Agency § 396. Copyright © 1958 by The American Law Institute.

Restatement of the Law, Contracts §§ 197, 365, 367, 370, 373, 374, 375, 376, 377(1), 384. Copyright © 1932 by The American Law Institute.

Restatement of the Law, Second, Contracts Tentative Draft Nos. 1–7, Revised and Edited § 222. Copyright © 1973 by The American Law Institute.

Restatement of the Law, Restitution §§ 142, 160, 162, 173(2), 188, 194, 201, 209, 210, 211. Copyright © 1937 by The American Law Institute.

Restatement of the Law, Torts § 913. Copyright © 1939 by The American Law Institute.

OUTLINE

OUTLINE

SECTION "B"

THE REMEDIES—HOW THEY ARE USED

IX. REMEDIES FOR INJURIES TO REALTY, PERSONAL PROPER-TY AND MONEY

X. REMEDIES FOR INJURIES TO PERSONAL INTERESTS

XI. REMEDIES FOR MISREPRESENTATION

XII. REMEDIES FOR MISTAKE

XIII. REMEDIES FOR DURESS, UN-DUE INFLUENCE AND RELAT-ED WRONGS

XIV. REMEDIES FOR BREACH OF CONTRACT

XV.   RESTITUTION FOR UNEN-FORCEABLE CONTRACTS

REMEDIES IN A NUTSHELL

SECOND EDITION

*

SECTION "A"

THE REMEDIES—WHAT THEY ARE

I. HISTORY OF REMEDIES

1. INTRODUCTION

To learn Remedies properly, one must know something of its historical background. The student is exposed to this material early in his legal study through such courses as Legal Methods, Legal Research, and Legal History. In addition, it is rare that in the discussion of any substantive area of law there is not also included a discussion of its own historical background. Many students find this type of discussion to be rather time-consuming and boring because it is usually not a subject for either law school or bar examinations. The student, however, overlooks the fact that history is an important element of a legal education and that many of the decisions being made today in the courts find their origins deep in the history of the subject itself. It is recognized that the student is most anxious to receive information and training in the "practice" of the law. While he is in law school, however, the emphasis should be on making him a legal scholar

[1]

while still equipping him with sufficient practitioner experience to enable him to take his place within the profession with a minimum of embarrassing transition.

In the not too distant past and continuing into many law schools today, Remedies did not exist as a separate subject. Rather, the curriculum covered this area with separate courses in Damages and Equity, with the greater emphasis being placed on Equity. In fact, this particular stress is prevalent today. Despite this, however, the student should know at the outset that the term "Remedies" refers to both legal and equitable actions. The student should also know at this time that generally he should examine the legal remedies first to see if they are adequate before proceeding to those in equity. It is only if they are inadequate at law that he will then turn to the equitable remedies themselves. While the specifics of whether or not a remedy is inadequate is discussed in subsequent chapters, it can be stated that there is no general or majority rule which one can cite to wrap the term "inadequate" into a nice, neat package for the student. Perhaps, it is in the same category as "unreasonable" which the courts have refused to define with any exactitude probably because the minute they do some sharp attorney will immediately figure a way around it. The student, however, should feel comfortable with the fact that case law concerning inadequacy has developed certain patterns which can be used as guidelines in making this determination. For example, whenever the plaintiff is seeking something which is unique in character such as land or a one-of-a-kind chattel, giving him money damages instead would certainly be inadequate. Another example would be where the plaintiff would have to bring a multiplicity of suits in order to get some degree of relief such as in a continuing trespass. While there does not seem to be as much emphasis on this criterion as there was in the early history of the common law, primarily because of the merger of law and equity today, courts do not hesitate to reach back to the very beginnings and apply that criterion in just about the same way as the Chancellors did at that time.

2. EARLY HISTORY OF EQUITY

The common law actions, as they developed originally, usually began with a petition from a peasant to the king asking for some form of relief caused by the oppressiveness of some feudal lord. The king would refer these to his Chancery for processing into what was called a "writ." This was, in effect, an authorization from the king to his court to hear the case. Since most of these petitions sought damages in the form of relief, the Chancery office forwarded them as a matter of routine; however, some petitions sought the recovery of a specific item itself such as land or a chattel. The Chancellor, instead of referring these, began to hear them himself on the grounds that the remedies at law were not adequate to restore or convey the specific property to the complainant. Once he made his decision, the Chancellor issued an order to the defendant to either do or not do a certain act "in the name of the king." Thus developed what has been

[3]

referred to constantly as "in personam" jurisdiction. If the defendant refused to obey the order, he was not in contempt of the Chancellor but rather of the king. From this seat of authority, therefore, developed the contempt powers of equity both civil and criminal.

a. Contempt Powers

Ordinarily, when one thinks of contempt, he immediately envisions the defendant doing something in the presence of the court which offends it. This is indeed one form of contempt and the judge before whom it is committed may find the defendant in contempt summarily without having any formal hearing. The reason is quite obvious. The judge must preserve the dignity of his court. If the contempt is committed outside of the presence of the court, it is a general rule that a full hearing must be held and if the charge is that of criminal contempt, the defendant must be protected by the rules of criminal procedure, including that of a right to a trial by jury. That right does not exist in civil contempt cases. As a guideline in determining whether or not a jury trial is required, one should look to the penalty itself. If it may be less than six months, the contempt is considered to be only a petty one for which no jury trial is required. If it exceeds that time, a jury trial is required.

Whenever the contempt powers are exercised, the defendant is usually given either a fine or a determinate prison sentence, although he may be given both where the violation of the decree is particularly flagrant. Decrees which require the defendant to take some specific type of action can be enforced by confining the defendant until he does comply. This is known as civil contempt in which case the defendant "has the keys to the jail door in his pocket." Confinement is not used, however, where the decree is to pay money because of constitutional and statutory prohibitions against imprisonment for debt. Not all decrees for money, however, are "debts", particularly those arising out of a statutory obligation such as alimony or child support cases, or those caused by fraud. Imprisonment for contempt of a prohibitory injunction is not imposed to force the defendant to comply but rather to punish him for disobeying the decree. In such cases, the contempt proceedings are regarded as criminal rather than civil and, in such cases, as noted above, the defendant must be protected by the rules of criminal procedure. The major distinction, therefore, between civil and criminal contempt, lies primarily in the proceedings used in both and the types of sentences imposed in each.

Who are the parties that are bound by a decree and thus subject to contempt proceedings if the decree is disobeyed? Federal Rule of Civil Procedure 65(d) makes the decree "binding only upon the parties to the action, their officers, agents, servants, employees, and attorneys, and upon those persons in active concert or participation with them who receive actual notice of the order by personal service or otherwise." As a basic rule, therefore, if a person is not a party to the action he should not be held in contempt for violating the decree particularly if he never had any notice of it.

At the common law, equity courts used an in rem theory to hold successors liable for any violation of the decree, by binding not only the defendant but also those in privity with them, such as "all successors and assigns." It would appear that Rule 65(d) prohibits the issuance of in rem injunctions; however, courts continue to issue them to protect their inherent ability to render a binding judgment.

As a general rule, an injunction which has been duly issued by a court of equity and properly served upon the persons who must observe it, must be obeyed by those persons however erroneous the action of the court was in issuing it. Until that decision is reversed for error by a higher court, the order must be respected and disobedience is contempt which is to be punished. There are jurisdictions, however, such as California, in which a defendant can challenge the validity of an injunction on the grounds that it was issued in excess of, or without, jurisdiction. In such a case, the defendant can elect to comply while seeking a judicial determination or he may disobey the order and raise his jurisdictional contentions when he is sought to be punished for such disobedience; however, in making this choice he maximizes his own peril. If it is determined that the decree was issued without or in excess of jurisdiction, his violation of the order constitutes no punishable wrong. If, however, the determination is otherwise, he may be punished. It must be emphasized, however, that this exception to the general rule is limited to the issue of the jurisdiction of the initial court in issuing the decree. In all other cases, and even in this one, the defendant takes the risk if he decides to disobey the order.

b. *Restitution*

Available in the early history of equity and still effective today, was restitution to give the plaintiff that which belonged to him. It was also available at law unless the legal title had passed to the defendant and it made no difference if the passage of the legal title was due to fraud, undue influence, or breach of a fiduciary relationship. Thus, the plaintiff could not get adequate relief at law and this is exactly why the Chancellor took jurisdiction in such instances. Where else was the plaintiff to go for a remedy when he was actually defrauded of his property so that legal title was passed to the fraudfeasor?

c. *Declaratory Judgments*

Declaratory relief was another remedy which was established early in equity to establish the right of the plaintiff in a given situation and it is so used today, particularly where the constitutionality of laws and ordinances are involved. A plaintiff will seek an injunction to test that constitutionality while asking for a declaration of his rights under that particular law or ordinance. It should be noted in declaratory judgment actions that the decree does not order that this be done or not done. So, there is no necessity for any follow-up process to the judgment. It does satisfy the rules of res judicata, however, because its termination is based upon the merits of the plaintiff's case. Its main value is to establish the legal rights of an individual in a particular situation where these may have been questioned, threatened, or disputed by another. Once the determination is made, that uncertainty and doubt will disappear with a favorable decree.

d. *In Personam vs. In Rem Jurisdiction*

As mentioned earlier, whenever the Chancellor operated directly on the parties, the jurisdiction was called "in personam." Originally, this was considered to be the major distinction between equity and law because law was supposed to act only in rem. Or, to put it another way, law did not act in personam. The distinction seems to be drawn too finely as an acceptable explanation. Under law procedures, the judgment of the court, for example, would be that A owes B a certain sum of money. This is not an in rem decision since it is not directed towards any property of A, but rather directly to A himself. Thus, at that particular point, the judgment is in personam because it concerns a personal liability. Moving now to the execution stage of the proceedings, if A does not pay B, the sheriff can enforce the judgment by levying upon property of A and selling as much of it as is necessary to satisfy the judgment. Thus, the execution is in rem while the judgment is in personam.

Where the matter is before a court of equity, the decree which issues is also an in personam one which is directed to the physical person of the defendant. Unlike law, however, the enforcement is also in personam in that the defendant is ordered to pay the sum of money involved. If the defendant disobeys the order, he may be subject to criminal contempt for that disobedience and also civil contempt to coerce him to make the payment. If he still refuses, equity can invoke a procedure of sequestration under which commissioners would be authorized to seize property of the defendant, sell it, and apply the proceeds to the payment of the debt. This, of course, was equivalent to the execution by the sheriff of a judgment at law. The question, therefore, naturally arises, doesn't equity by acting in personam also reach the res? For example, the ideal situation in equity is to have both the parties and the res before it in which case equity can order the defendant to convey the res itself. The second ideal situation would be to have the parties before equity even though the res may be in a foreign jurisdiction because the decree can still order the defendant to convey the res. The most difficult situation is where the defendant is not before the court and neither is the res. Here, it is almost impossible for the court to issue an in personam order since it lacks jurisdiction over the defendant. If the res, however, is before the court, but the defendant is not, equity can issue a conveyance through a decretal transfer of the res to the plaintiff provided constructive service has been made upon the defendant; or the court may simply attach the property which would give the court a quasi-in-rem jurisdiction under which the property would be sold. The majority rule in such a situation, therefore, is that when the jurisdiction is quasi-in-rem and is based upon service of process which is constructive, the decree is that of a decretal transfer of title rather than an in personam order of the court. One may ask just what is the difference since the effect seems to be the same? The difference is that the defendant cannot be subject to any contempt procedures for not obeying the decree and if he should sell the property to a bona fide purchaser for value before the plaintiff records the decretal transfer, the sale will be a valid one.

In summary, since the jurisdictional issue is of such vital importance, if the res and both of the parties are before the court, this is the ideal situation for in personam jurisdiction. If the res and the vendee are before the court, constructive notice can be given to the vendor and as long as the vendor's land is before the court, this will give equity a quasi-in-rem jurisdiction so that a decretal transfer of the property can be made to the vendee. If, however, the vendor and his property are before the court but the vendee is not, or, if the contract is one for personal services, constructive notice will not suffice to satisfy the requirement for in personam jurisdiction and any decree issued without the presence of the defendant is void and unenforceable. Finally, what is the rule where the court has the parties before it but the res is located in another jurisdiction? Equity can order the parties to convey and pay because of the in personam jurisdiction. In other words, equity can grant specific performance. But does that affect the land in the other jurisdiction? The answer is in the negative and is still the same even if a deed is executed by an officer of the court. The affected party, however, can sue upon it in the foreign jurisdiction but it does not have the full faith and credit clause behind it because it affects title to local land.

Speaking of the full faith and credit clause, just what is the rule with respect to equity decrees? The majority rule, and this by a slim majority, is that equity decrees for the conveyance of land in foreign jurisdictions and for the recognition of foreign money decrees, must be given full faith and credit by a sister state. This does not mean that the courts in the sister state must issue execution on the judgment but they must consider it to be res judicata and allow the maintenance of an action on the judgment.

There are also jurisdictions which apply what might well be referred to as the "liberal minority rule" in that foreign jurisdictions would render comity to such decrees provided that the law of the situs and the law of the jurisdiction granting the decree are substantially the same; however, it is not entitled to full faith and credit. Finally, there would be the minority rule that a foreign decree is not entitled to full faith and credit at the situs and will not be recognized there.

3. SPECIFIC AREARS OF EARLY EQUITY JURISDICTION

a. Uses and Trusts

Under the English law, when the owner of land died, it passed to his eldest son who paid an inheritance tax to the lord. As one would expect, owners of land figured a way around this by transferring the land to a group of friends who held the title by agreeing to use the land as the owner wished. This avoided the payment of the inheritance tax and was called a "Use". This practice continued until 1535 when Henry VIII, who was losing the taxes, had Parliament pass the Statute of Uses which provided that the beneficiary of the use would be deemed to hold the legal estate. Equity entered the picture by first holding that the Statute did not affect "active uses". An "active use" occurred when the owner, instead of just remaining in possession, required his friends to do something affirmative with the property such as taking some of the profits and investing them. This made the friends (feofees) "trustees" and the owner became a beneficiary with an equitable ownership. Another way was to validate a passive trust, e.g., when the Statute of Uses came into existence, it executed the Use, i.e., it gave legal title from A to B. If, however, the conveyance said "from A to B to hold for the use of C", even though the Statute would execute the title in B, the Chancellor said that B in good conscience must convey to C because B held as a trustee for the benefit of C.

b. *Mortgages*

If a person wanted to borrow money at the common law and desired to use his land as security, the mortgagor had to make an absolute deed to the mortgagee with a covenant that the mortgagee would reconvey when payment was made when due. If it was not made at that time, the mortgagor lost his property but was still liable on the debt and even if later he made full payment, he could not get his land back. The Chancellor held that the land was merely security for the debt and as long as the mortgagor paid within a reasonable time after default, the mortgagee must reconvey; however, if the mortgagor failed to pay within a reasonable time, the mortgagee could go into equity himself and ask for a foreclosure of the mortgagor's right of redemption.

4. REQUIREMENT FOR JURY TRIAL

The above discussion is sufficient background at this point to demonstrate the position of the Chancellor and his role in the development of equity. At the outset, however, it is important to understand that the majority of states today have integrated equitable and legal actions. Separate courts of equity exist in only a few states and these are Arkansas, Delaware, Mississippi, and Tennessee. In other states such as Iowa, Maryland, Massachusetts, New Jersey, Oregon, Pennsylvania and Virginia, equity is administered in the same court as law but on a different side of it. In all others, equity is administered in the same court and by the same procedure as law. The Federal Rules of Civil Procedure (28 U.S.C.A.) Rules 1 and 2, provide that there shall be one form of action in both law or in equity known as "civil action." There is one area, however, at the federal level which prevents complete integration and that is the requirement of trial by jury in civil cases at law. Equity perennially has operated without a jury, and in many instances, this is advantageous to the plaintiff and one of the main reasons for seeking equity jurisdiction. It also has another important effect. If a jury trial is not required, most judges do not hesitate to reach into the substantive laws of either law or equity to decide the case. Care must be taken however, where there is a constitutional right to a trial by jury. Historically and presently, equity is prominent for its non-jury trials; however, what if both legal and equitable issues arise in the same case? One obvious approach is to treat the issues separately as law and equity did originally before the merger took place. Under this approach, the legal issues would be decided at law with a jury trial, followed by the equitable actions. Another approach is to look at the remedy itself to determine whether the action will be equitable or legal and decide accordingly. There is also a third approach which seems to be followed by the federal courts which is based upon the rationalization that a case is not essentially equitable or essentially legal. Under this approach, if there are legal issues in a case, they must be decided as such and first. Further, if a legal issue arises later in the case, it also must be decided under legal rules, i.e., a jury trial. Thus, in such instances, the court must impanel a jury to hear the legal issue and once this has been determined, the trial can continue as an equitable one.

It is important also to know at this point that even though the judge decides initially to hear the case in equity, he may continue to resolve it completely even though legal rather than equitable relief will be granted. This has been referred to as the "clean-up" doctrine and was used originally in equity to preclude a jury trial on the legal issues which were treated as incidental to the equitable claim. It has one major advantage in that it reduces multiple litigation; however, care should be taken when dealing with the federal courts where the majority rule is to treat the equitable actions as incidental to the legal so that the right to a jury trial is preserved. Where this rule is not followed in the state courts, the clean-up doctrine may allow the equity court to decide the legal issues as well as the equitable, but it may deprive the defendant of a jury trial. The better approach would be to allow the clean-up doctrine but if legal issues are involved in an equitable action, a jury should be impaneled to hear those issues and be dissolved once those issues are resolved.

5. DEFENSES IN EQUITY

The standard defenses in equity have been those of laches and unclean hands. There are others which are peculiar to certain equitable actions such as, for example, in a suit for specific performance, where the defenses could be the Statute of Frauds, mistake, misrepresentation, or estoppel. These are discussed in Chapter VIII on Specific Performance.

a. Laches

The first point to grasp with respect to laches is that it applies to all equitable actions and occurs when a party has delayed the assertion of his claim unreasonably so as to result in a prejudice to the other party because of the delay. Where this is so, equity will deny relief to the party guilty of the laches. It must be emphasized, however, that the doctrine does involve two elements: unreasonable delay by the plaintiff and prejudice to the defendant. Early in its history, Chancery developed the doctrine that where the plaintiff in equity delayed beyond the period of the statute applicable at law, relief would be refused on the ground of laches even though no specific prejudice to the defendant was shown. Today, in most states there are statutes of limitations applying to suits in equity. Despite these, however, the doctrine still holds that even if the delay is for a shorter period of time than that of the statute, it may still bar equitable relief if it is unreasonable and prejudicial to the defendant. As an example, the defense of laches in a suit for specific performance is to be considered wholly independent of the Statute of Limitations. Even if the action is brought within the period prescribed by the statute, if it has been so delayed as to preclude the granting of equitable relief, the plaintiff will be referred to law for damages. The rationalization for the doctrine is found in the well-settled principle that where a person stands by and sees another committing an act which he feels infringes on his rights and fails to assert his title or right, he will be estopped from asserting it later.

Laches begins to run from the time the plaintiff has the knowledge that one of his rights has been infringed. There are no precise rules governing its application and each case is determined by its own circumstances; however, one important guideline is predominant viz., laches is concerned more with the effect of the passing of time than with the mere passage of time as represented by the equitable maxim "Equity aids the vigilant, not those who slumber on their rights."

b. Unclean Hands

As with the defense of laches, the doctrine of "unclean hands" applies to all equitable actions. Its short title is derived from the equitable maxim "He who comes into equity must come with clean hands." At first glance this would seem to demand that the parties cannot use equity unless they are both pure in mind and body. This, of course, is not the correct interpretation. The maxim confines itself to the "hands" which cannot be dirtied with respect to the rights which the plaintiff is trying to assert against the defendant. For example, if the plaintiff is guilty of fraud, illegality or of some form of tortious conduct with respect to the matter being litigated, equity will not give him relief either through injunction or specific performance. Equity has always refused specific performance of a contract which has been obtained by unfair dealings on the part of the plaintiff such as by overreaching or concealing important facts; in other words, using sharp and unscrupulous practices which are offensive to good conscience and the dictates of natural justice. It must be emphasized, however, that the uncleanness must arise out of the same transaction on which the plaintiff is suing. The court will not go outside of the case to examine the conduct of the plaintiff in other matters or to try to find out just what his general reputation is with respect to fair dealings.

6. EQUITABLE SERVITUDES

Historically, the law has always provided several ways in which an individual can impose restrictions on the use of land whether he owned it or not. These are called "equitable servitudes" which are intended to bind successive owners while benefiting the grantor. The best examples are injunctions against nuisances on the land of another, easements, or covenants which run with the property. Once the servitude attaches to the property, any one who purchases with notice of that equity cannot stand in a different situation than the party from whom he purchased. If, however, he is a bona fide purchaser for value who takes without notice of the servitude, it cannot be enforced against him. Such a situation would be rare in this country because of the constructive notice to which vendees are subject by the land recording system in use throughout the United States.

For the purposes of interpretation, just how are these servitudes viewed by the courts of equity? If, for example, a covenant is made that the property, or a certain portion of it, cannot be used for grazing, or farming, or for horse racing, or for motor cycling, or for any similar reason, does this mean that the property is so permanently restricted? Or, is it personal to the covenantor? Is it just a contract between the covenantor and covenantee or is it an interest in land which brings in the Statute of Frauds? The majority view seems to be that courts construe such covenants strictly because they do favor the free use of land. Some jurisdictions look upon the restrictions as contracts concerning the use of the land which is personal to the covenantor and where this interpretation is given, the Statute of Frauds does not apply. Where it is viewed as actually establishing an interest in the land itself, then, of course, the Statute of Frauds would be applied together with its exceptions. The courts will not enforce restrictions which are either illegal or restrain trade. For example, in the not too distant past, restrictive covenants were made to keep certain racial groups and individuals out of certain areas. It was determined finally that such restrictions denied those members equal protection of the laws and further that damages would not be awarded where such covenants were breached. In other words, the covenants can be made, but they will not be enforced for these reasons and because they are basically against public policy.

Is there any way of terminating servitudes? The most obvious way, of course, is by mutual agreement of the parties, even where groups may be involved. Or, the property may change so greatly because of changes in the locality or environment that the servitude is no longer able to produce the benefit which it originally intended to accomplish. One has only to examine the population explosions with their attendant changes in the development of large apartment complexes, massive shopping centers particularly in the suburban areas, urban renewal itself, new zoning rules, and other such major changes which would have an impact on a restrictive covenant made in the past for an entirely different purpose.

[19]

7. THE MAXIMS OF EQUITY

Any preliminary discussion of equity and its jurisdiction would be incomplete unless some reference was made to the "maxims of equity" which have developed over the years. They tend to cover the entire field of equity; however, this is an almost impossible task. Nevertheless, the courts do use them and usually in one of two ways: enabling or restrictive. The enabling pertain to the subject of equitable jurisdiction and the granting of relief, whereas, the restrictive causes the court to deny relief. The most common are:

(a) "He who seeks equity must do equity." The plaintiff cannot expect to receive equitable relief unless he shows he is making provision to handle any equitable claims of the defendant.

(b) "He who comes into equity must come with clean hands." This is also known as the "clean hands doctrine" which is a defense in all equitable actions.

(c) "Equity aids the vigilant, not those who slumber on their rights." This is also called "laches" which is another defense in all equitable actions.

(d) "Equity acts in personam." This is the preferred basis for equitable jurisdiction.

(e) "Equity follows the law." This is an important cliché which students frequently overlook by failing first to establish the substantive law involved, whether tort or contract, before proceeding to a discussion of the applicable remedy.

(f) "Equity delights to do justice and not by halves." This is the basis for the "clean-up" doctrine under which once equity assumes jurisdiction, it will hear the case to the very end even if a legal remedy is involved.

(g) "Equity will not suffer a wrong to be without a remedy." This is the basis for the oft-repeated statement that "for every wrong there is a remedy."

(h) "Equity regards that done which ought to be done." The doctrine of equitable conversion rests on this maxim.

(i) "Equity regards substance rather than form."

(j) "Equity imputes an intent to fulfill an obligation."

(k) "Equality is equity."

(*l*) "Between equal equities the law will prevail." This is applied in the bona fide purchaser rule where the trustee without authority sells trust property to an innocent purchaser.

(m) "Between equal equities the first in order of time will prevail." This is invoked where both parties have equitable interests and neither has legal title.

(n) "Equity abhors a forfeiture."

(*o*) "Equity will not aid a volunteer."

II. BASIC RULES FOR LEGAL AND EQUITABLE REMEDIES

1. INTRODUCTION

The purpose of this chapter is to provide, in a succinct and summary form, the remedies which are available either at law or in equity.

The reason for this approach is to acquaint the student immediately with the scope of the subject while at the same time isolating for him the specific remedies he is required to know. The most common complaint of students in a Remedies course is the early identification of the remedies themselves. They see before them a mass and volume of case law coupled with a complex application of seemingly endless rules. Once they recognize that there are only certain specific forms of relief available, they move very quickly to absorb the intricacies of each. As the subjects which follow will demonstrate, these basic rules are applied in most situations with certain modifications to fit the specific area being treated. Depending upon that situation, therefore, the student can develop his own checklist of available remedies and apply it accordingly. There is one caveat, however, which cannot be stressed too many times: before considering the available remedy, make sure that the substantive law involved is clear and understood. This is important because of the fundamental rule that the remedy follows the substantive law.

2. BASIC REMEDIES

The basic remedies are: Compensatory Damages, Restitution, Rescission, Reformation, Specific Performance and Injunction. Each will be summarized in this chapter and will be treated in greater detail in the following chapters.

a. *Compensatory Damages*

This is the basic legal remedy which has only one goal: to make good the losses of the plaintiff. It is known as a substitutionary remedy because money usually substitutes for property. On the other hand, if it is property that is to be recovered, it is referred to as an "in specie" remedy. Included in the term Compensatory Damages are those referred to as General, Special, Nominal, and Punitive.

b. *Restitution*

Unlike Compensatory Damages which is to recover money for the losses incurred by the plaintiff, the goal of Restitution is to reach the "gains" of the defendant and to prevent his unjust enrichment. It is available in such actions as quasi-contract, replevin, ejectment, and constructive trust.

c. *Rescission*

This is a restitutionary contract remedy which is designed to "undo" the contract. It puts the parties back where they were before the contract was formed, provided this is still possible to do. It is used generally in situations involving fraud, mutual mistake, and illegality. One of the first things to realize about this remedy is that it can be applied by the parties outside of the courts through their own mutual agreement to rescind. If court action is required, it can either be at law or in equity.

d. Reformation

Unlike Rescission which has as its object to "undo" the contract, the purpose of Reformation is to "keep" the contract. It is used by the court to make the contract conform to the intention of the parties when the contract was formed. It is used generally where mistake or fraud is present.

e. Specific Performance

This is an equitable remedy in contracts which is designed to compel the defendant to do what he promised he would with the plaintiff. While its application is discretionary, it is used primarily in land contracts or if personalty is involved, then only where it is unique.

f. Injunction

This is an equitable remedy in either contract or tort which orders the defendant to do (mandatory) or not to do (prohibitory or preventive) a certain thing. Like specific performance, its application is discretionary; however, it is applied carefully by the courts because of its power and effect upon a person or his property.

3. ANCILLARY REMEDIES

In addition to the basic remedies outlined above, equity has available to it certain ancillary remedies which are included in this chapter for the general information of the student. States differ on the requirements for these on bar examinations and it is recommended that students contact their own Committee of Bar Examiners for this determination.

a. *Writ of Ne Exeat*

This was an old latin writ which was used to prevent a person from leaving the kingdom to escape his liabilities. It was used initially in the common law to prevent members of the clergy in England from departing the realm to visit the Pope. Later, it was applied to the subjects of the king who would try to depart from the realm rather than remain and fight for him. Finally, it was applied to private rights, particularly where the departure would deprive the plaintiff of his in personam relief. Today, it is used primarily for the enforcement of equitable pecuniary demands and to prevent the threatened departure of a husband who is trying to avoid the payment of alimony.

b. · *Equitable Receiverships*

These are brought to appoint a receiver during a trial to hold the property of the defendant where there is a concern that he might dispose of it rather than have it used to pay a judgment. Generally, there has to be some immediate threat or information that the property will be lost, destroyed, or squandered before a receiver is appointed. The main reason for not ordering the action without such a consideration is that it takes the property of the defendant before a final determination as to liability is made. Thus, there is a definite interference with the right of the defendant with respect to his own property which should not be treated lightly by the courts.

c. *Bills of Peace*

Originally, this procedure was used where many plaintiffs had similar claims at law against the one defendant. Today, the reverse seems to be the case. It is now used where the defendant is being sued by multiple parties in actions at law. In such a case, the defendant may ask in a bill of peace that all of the plaintiffs be joined because common issues of law and fact are involved and it will probably save litigation. Otherwise, he would be faced with a multiplicity of suits, particularly where a plaintiff harasses a single defendant with multiple suits on the same cause of action. To prevent this, the Bill of Peace has been codified by what are called "vexatious litigant" statutes. Also, today, many of the former suits under a Bill of Peace are now covered by rules of joinder and class actions. In any case, the individual rights, particularly those requiring a trial by jury, should be examined to see if the one trial is the proper course of action.

d. *Interpleader and Bills of Interpleader*

This remedy arises when an individual is confronted with diverse claims about the same property which he holds. Where this occurs, the defendant can bring the property into equity, obtain an injunction against the suits of the claimants and compel them to plead their own claims in equity. Usually there are four requirements before the action can be brought: (1) the same item has to be claimed by the adverse parties; (2) their claims are derived from a common source; (3) the holder of the property has no claim or interest in it; and (4) the holder has no liability to either of the claimants. At the federal level, The Interpleader Act and Federal Rule 22 have eliminated the four conditions for interpleader actions mentioned above. Where a holder of the property seeks interpleader to avoid the adverse claims, his recovery of costs, expenses and attorney's fees is discretionary with the court.

e. Bills Quia Timet

Originally, these actions were brought to forestall future injury or damage. Before it could succeed, the plaintiff had to show that the danger was immediate or imminent and that the damage itself would be very substantial, if not irreparable. What the situation boiled down to basically was that if and when the damage did occur, it would happen in such a way that the plaintiff would not be able to protect himself against it. When this was proven, the bill of quia timet would be granted. Today, it is fairly limited to the situation where a negotiable instrument in the hands of a defendant is sought to be canceled before he can give it to a bona fide purchaser for value. If, however, the instrument is void on its face, the plaintiff cannot be hurt, so the relief will not be given. This is a good example, however, of the application of the remedy because he knows he will suffer damage if and when the defendant does give the instrument to a BFP.

f. Bill to Remove Cloud From Title

It is a standard rule that one who is the owner of real property even though he is not in possession of it, can bring a suit in equity to remove any cloud on the title of it, otherwise, the plaintiff would have to bring repeated ejectment actions at law. What is sought is to reform or cancel records or to correct deeds, and for this reason neither their possession nor the right to it is a prerequisite to seeking the remedy which today is largely statutory.

g. Writs of Assistance

Whenever possession rather than title is in issue, equity can issue an in personam order enjoining the defendant to give up possession to the plaintiff. If this is not effective, equity can issue a Writ of Assistance to the sheriff to then put the plaintiff in possession. At the federal level, there is the All Writs Act (28 U.S.C.A. § 1651a) which provides that "the Supreme Court and all courts established by Congress may issue all writs necessary in aid of their respective jurisdiction and agreeable to the usages and principles of law." In addition, Rule 70 of the Federal Rules of Civil Procedure provides that the Writ of Assistance can be issued by the clerk of the court.

h. *Writs of Sequestration*

Whenever the defendant received a decree ordering him to do a certain thing, he could be imprisoned for his failure to obey the order and also by remaining in jail, he could be coerced through civil contempt to comply with the order. But if he chose to stay in jail, what could equity do? Originally, equity did nothing but let the defendant remain in jail; however, this did not give the plaintiff his relief, so equity appointed sequestrators at the request of the plaintiff through a writ of sequestration to seize possession of the defendant's chattels. At first, this was all that was done in order to try to coerce the defendant to comply. Where this failed, equity then extended the writ to the sale of his chattels. At the federal level, Rule 70 of the Federal Rules of Civil Procedure provides that the "clerk shall issue a writ of sequestration against the property of the disobedient party to compel obedience to the judgment."

i. *Appointment of Masters and Commissioners*

The use of masters, referees, and commissioners of a court of equity has been in existence for a long time. When appointed, these officers can act as masters in chancery and as such, they can determine facts, hold hearings, make decisions, all of which are subject to the control of the appointing court. At the federal level, Rule 53 of the Federal Rules of Civil Procedure allows a district court to appoint a master or special master whose duties may be that of a referee, auditor, or examiner. One of the most common examples is the Voting Rights Acts which usually provides for the appointment of referees and/or masters to supervise the conduct of an election. The student should always consider this authority by a court of equity when the question of supervision or enforceability of a decree arises. Frequently, rather than concluding that it would be impracticable for equity to enforce the decree, the appointment of an agent of the court may provide the necessary solution.

III. INJUNCTIONS

1. INTRODUCTION

One of the major benefits accruing from equity jurisdiction was its enforcement powers which strengthened its decrees given by an in personam order to the defendant telling him to do or not to do a certain thing. This type of decree is known as an "injunction." When it is issued, it can enjoin the defendant *not* to do a specific act. This is then called a "prohibitory" type of injunction. If, on the other hand, it enjoins him to do something affirmative, it is called a "mandatory" type of injunction.

A mandatory injunction is one that compels the defendant to restore things to their former condition and virtually directs him to perform an act. The court when it sees that a wrong has been committed, has a right at once to put an end to it and has no hesitation in doing so by a mandatory injunction. While these are the two major types of classifications, there are also three other forms of injunctions used by equity: permanent, preliminary, and the temporary restraining order (TRO).

The permanent injunction is one which is issued as a final solution to the matter under dispute. It does not mean that it can never be reversed or modified. It means simply that after a full hearing of all of the factors involved, the decision has been made to make the injunction a permanent one. This is opposed by the preliminary (or interlocutory) injunction which is granted before a full hearing can be held. The procedure involved is usually an informal one consisting of the following:

(a) The defendant is given notice of the hearing on the motion for the preliminary injunction.

(b) The plaintiff must post a bond to protect the defendant if the preliminary injunction cannot be upheld.

(c) The hearing itself is usually informal and precedes the final full hearing on the injunction because of the emergency nature of the motion for a preliminary injunction.

The temporary restraining order (TRO) is far more serious because the injunction is issued without notice to the defendant. It is not only because of the emergency nature of the situation, but also because the requirement for relief is so urgent that there is no time even for a preliminary hearing. The plaintiff must post a security bond in the same manner as for the preliminary injunction. Because of the fact that the TRO is issued without notice to the defendant, it is a very limited form of injunction and is issued usually for a period not in excess of 10 days. As far as the defendant is concerned, he is not bound by the order until he receives actual notice of it and he can ask immediately for a review of the order with or without a stay of the order. In the case of a prohibitory injunction, these are not stayed because of an appeal; whereas, mandatory injunctions are automatically stayed for that reason.

Equity places certain additional safeguards around both the preliminary injunctions and the temporary restraining orders for the very reason that the defendant's full exposure is really delayed until the final full hearing is held. In other words, one should envision the process to begin with the temporary restraining order in which the defendant is not even present and then move to the preliminary injunction in which he is present but which, because of its informality and still apparent emergency nature, favors the plaintiff, to the full and final hearing at which the defendant will be given full opportunity to present his side of the situation. It is because of this procedure that neither the preliminary injunction nor the temporary restraining order are granted unless the injury threatened to the plaintiff is irreparable. For example, suppose the defendant mistakenly believes that certain valuable trees are located on his property whereas in fact they are located on the land of the plaintiff and the defendant, in that belief, contracts with a firm to enter the land the next morning and cut down these trees. Unless there is a device such as the temporary restraining order which can be granted under emergency conditions the injury would cause irreparable harm to the plaintiff in this particular respect.

The concept of irreparable injury in equity traces back to the early assumption of jurisdiction by the Chancellor to enjoin waste, continuing trespass, and nuisance. Irreparable injury is suffered where monetary damages are difficult to ascertain or are inadequate. The word "irreparable" means that which cannot be repaired, retrieved, put down again, atoned for. For example, the cutting down of ornamental trees. Even a trespass can be irreparable when from its nature, it is impossible to make full and complete reparation in damages. For example, if the trespass is continuous in its nature and its repetition is threatened, equity, although each act of trespass, if taken by itself would not be destructive of the property and the legal remedy would be adequate if each act stood alone, will prevent the threatened wrong by injunction, because the injured party has not a complete and adequate remedy by one action at law for the entire wrong, while a court of equity, by preventing the wrong, affords in a single action a complete remedy. The granting or refusal of a preliminary injunction, whether mandatory or preventive, calls for the exercise of a sound judicial discretion in view of all of the circumstances of the particular case. Regard should be had to the nature of the controversy, the object for which the injunction is sought, the comparative hardship to the respective parties and the probability of the plaintiff's ultimate success on the merits. The legitimate object of a preliminary injunction, preventive in nature, is the preservation of the property or rights in controversy, the object for which the injunction is sought and the comparative hardship or inconvenience to the respective parties involved in the awarding or denial of the injunction. The legitimate object of a preliminary injunction, preventive in nature, is the preservation of the property or rights in controversy until the decision of the case on a full and final hearing upon the merits, or the dismissal of the bill for want of jurisdiction or other sufficient cause. The balance of convenience or hardship ordinarily is a factor of controlling importance in cases of substantial doubt existing at the time of granting or refusing the preliminary injunction. Such doubt may relate either to the facts or to the law, or to both. Where, for instance, the effect of the injunction would be disastrous to an established and legitimate business through its destruction or interruption in whole or in part, strong and convincing proof of right on the part of the complainant and of the urgency of his case is necessary to justify an exercise of the injunctive power.

2. SPECIFIC REQUIREMENTS FOR INJUNCTIONS

Case law in the area of injunctions has established that they will not be granted without complying with certain prerequisites. These elements are: TORT (or other cause of action), ADEQUACY OF THE REMEDY AT LAW, ENFORCEABILITY, PROPERTY RIGHT, BALANCING THE HARDSHIPS and DEFENSES. These elements are designed to enable either the student or the practitioner to develop his own checklist in order to satisfy himself that he does or does not have the equitable basis required for such a powerful remedy.

a. *The tort (or other cause of action)*

Since the remedy usually follows the substantive law, the first thing that has to be identified is the specific tort itself or the appropriate cause of action. Case law in this area identifies the most commonly used as the unfair competition torts such as infringements of trademarks or trade names, theft of trade secrets, interference with contractual relations, and inducing the breach of a contract. Others commonly used are nuisance, defamation, trespass and invasion of the right of privacy. For example, if trademarks or trade names are involved, the distinction between the two will be important. A trademark must be affixed to the goods involved while a trade name is one which has become associated with the goods themselves. Trade names do not have to be affixed to the item but the name itself must have acquired a secondary meaning, i.e., a meaning to the public as to the source of the goods. It is the association by the public of the article with the reliability and quality of the manufacturer. This is the property right which equity seeks to protect. Once this property right is established, the situations should be examined to see just where the infringement has occurred. Ordinarily, it will occur if one person uses the trade name in his business or in a manner which causes confusion in the mind of the buyer. Once the infringement is established, the prospective purchasers should be examined. If they are experts who know the difference between the source of the two products, the infringement or injury will be slight. If, on the other hand, they are of the normal public who have become confused by the sudden appearance of another similar item, the damage could be serious, and the fact that the defendant is not in direct competition is immaterial. An individual should be able to protect his own trade name in his business.

If trade secrets are involved, one of the first questions asked should be: is the list a confidential one? Or, is it available to any one? If, in fact, it is a limited list, the chances are that it will be protected; whereas, if it is a general one, it will not. Herein lies the property interest which equity is looking to protect. But what if there are two lists, one written and one non-written? Ordinarily, the non-written list will not be protected. If there is a fiduciary duty involved, the lists will be protected without establishing a specific property right. As far as the injunction itself is concerned, can the plaintiff enjoin the ex-employee only or also his new boss? Ordinarily, the injunction will cover both; however, it will only restrict him (or them) from soliciting the customers directly; not from doing business with them. In other words, the defendants cannot go out to get the customers but they can come in to him.

Where the tort concerns an interference with contractual relations, just how the interference was accomplished should be examined. This is a tort designed to induce a refusal to deal. Was it accomplished by violence or only by oral suggestion? Was it an actual contract or just a business relationship? Who was involved—a lawyer, a competitor, or just a stranger? What are the interests on each side? Was the inducement or interference privileged? A competitor's privilege is most important because he can improve his own position by inducing a refusal to deal with another competitor but he cannot induce him to breach a contract.

Where nuisance is involved, there is a concern because of an unreasonable interference with the use and enjoyment of one's property. Normally, nuisance is one of two types—public or private. Ordinarily, equity will not enjoin public nuisances, unless the action is brought by a public official, because such nuisances usually affect a large number of persons who are similarly affected by the nuisance. A private person can seek to enjoin a public nuisance but only if he is able to show that his injuries are substantially different than those suffered by the average member of the public, e.g., the blocked area deprives only him of access to his driveway. In other words, he would have to show special damages. Other examples would be where the defendant builds a chemical plant next to the plaintiff and because of the noxious fumes, the plaintiff becomes ill. Or if the plaintiff has access to certain water rights, and the defendant's plant begins to pollute the stream.

Defamation can occur either personally where the plaintiff's reputation is injured or by commercial disparagement or trade libel where customers no longer want to deal with the merchant. In the case of personal defamation, unless it is either libel or slander per se, the plaintiff is required to prove his special damages first. Close consideration should be given to the distinction between defamation and invasion of the right of privacy and to whether or not any constitutional issues are involved arising under the First Amendment guarantee of freedom of the press. Equity is most reluctant to enjoin the publication of articles because of this Amendment.

b. *Inadequacy of the Remedy at Law*

As noted even in Chapter I, dealing with the history of equity jurisdiction, the Chancellor began to hear cases because the remedy at law was "inadequate." For example, suppose that real estate is involved and the plaintiff is seeking to eject the defendant from his (plaintiff's) property. Ejectment at law, once the title is established in the plaintiff, may appear to be an adequate remedy. But what if the sheriff either won't or can't execute the judgment. In such a case, is the remedy at law really adequate? Or if the subject matter is a chattel, would an action at law in replevin to recover the chattel be adequate? It would unless the item was a unique one. Further, the action at law does provide for the plaintiff to be able to obtain the chattel immediately pending the final outcome of the trial; however, the defendant also has an opportunity to present his reasons for holding the article at an informal hearing. Both parties are required to post bond to ensure the appearance of the article at the final hearing. If the item was unique, however, such as a stamp or coin collection, the plaintiff would not be interested in money damages because he could not replace the collection. Or, if the damages are actually too hard to estimate because, for example, the chattel has a special sentimental value to the plaintiff which cannot be measured adequately, then the remedy at law would be inadequate.

The major reasons for inadequacy of the remedy at law are: LAND IS UNIQUE; CHATTEL IS UNIQUE; BREACH OF A FIDUCIARY RELATIONSHIP; MULTIPLICITY OF SUITS; DAMAGES ARE TOO SPECULATIVE; and, A FAR SUPERIOR REMEDY AVAILABLE ONLY IN EQUITY (such as a Bill of Accounting or Reformation). For example, threatened trespasses could result in a multiplicity of suits none of which would order that the trespasses be discontinued. Giving money damages, probably nominal at best, would be a very unsatisfactory and inadequate remedy. The plaintiff wants the trespasses to stop. He also wants only one suit in which to achieve this objective. Since this cannot be obtained at law, his only recourse is equity.

If the item is a unique one, such as the coin collection described above, what is the actual loss in terms of money to the plaintiff? How are these measured? True, expert opinion and current market values may be some indication; however, what about the personal value to the plaintiff of such a collection? What of the effort he put into the process of collecting these rare coins? The answers to these questions put the damages in a very highly speculative area. Where this is the case and thus the damages are too difficult to determine, the remedy at law would be inadequate.

If the injury would be an irreparable one, such as the threatened removal of valuable trees from the plaintiff's property and these trees are of a type which could not be replaced, then the remedy at law in the form of money damages would be inadequate. As a general rule, if the chattel is a unique one or real estate is involved, the injury is usually irreparable because neither can be replaced. Further, generally, where the injury is one which has been threatened rather than committed, the remedy at law would be inadequate because none would exist. The only recourse would be to equity to issue an injunction to prevent the threat from materializing. However, equity does refrain from issuing injunctions for purely prospective torts where the threat has, in fact, ceased.

Finally, despite the fact that a remedy does exist at law, the one in equity may be so far superior that in all good conscience it would be used. For example, if the injury to the plaintiff may be compensated in money damages but still impose upon him a duty of doing something additional, then is the remedy adequate? Suppose that the defendant has blocked the driveway of the plaintiff with debris. Is money damages adequate where the plaintiff still has the duty to have the debris removed? Or wouldn't it be a far superior remedy for the plaintiff to obtain an injunction from equity ordering the defendant to remove the debris himself?

c. *Can the Decree be Enforced or Supervised?*

It can be taken as a general principle that equity does not want to issue orders which are difficult to enforce or supervise. The reason is that in many situations, the court does not possess the expertise necessary to determine whether or not the defendant is actually complying with the injunction as he should. This is not a difficulty with prohibitory injunctions because if the defendant fails to comply, the court can simply cite him for contempt and punish him. On the other hand, if the injunction is a mandatory one which is ordering the defendant to do a specific act, the court has to take into consideration the necessity of supervising the defendant to ensure compliance. This is one of the reasons that equity hesitates to issue mandatory injunctions in building contractor cases. How could it supervise the contractor adequately? Where would it obtain the expertise to know whether or not the contractor is in fact doing a good job? It is also for this reason that the courts prefer to issue the prohibitory injunction—the feasibility of enforcement is much simpler. One of the favorite examples in this respect is the enforcement of negative covenants in contracts of employment. In these, the employee agrees to work only for the employer and for no others, usually because of his unique talents and services to the employer. If for some reason, the employee should want to breach that contract, equity will not issue a mandatory injunction that he remain working for the original employer because it would be difficult to supervise and would violate the employee's right under the Thirteenth Amendment. It is much easier to enforce the negative covenant by issuing a prohibitory injunction that the employee cannot work for any other person.

Another problem which occurs with respect to feasibility of enforcement or supervision arises where the decree would operate in another state.

Can equity effectively enforce or supervise a decree which orders a defendant to do something in another jurisdiction? What power do they have over the defendant to supervise his actions while he is in the other jurisdiction? Originally, they avoided the problem by simply not issuing such decrees, on the grounds that they did not have either the power or the authority to issue them. The real reason, however, was the lack of feasibility of enforcement. Today, equity courts make a distinction between their power to issue the decree and their ability to enforce it. They now claim that they have such power even if the enforcement is not feasible. One way of doing this is to require the defendant to put up a bond in the state in which the decree is issued or to send the defendant with a receiver appointed by the court to go to the second state with a decree to act.

d. *What are the Property Rights of the Individuals?*

Before answering this question, it is necessary to comment briefly on the requirement for a property right before equity will grant injunctive relief. Originally equity did require that a property right would have to be established before equity could attach some form of relief to it. The plaintiff could not just come into equity to enforce his personal rights. For example, if the plaintiff sued the defendant for trademark or trade name infringement, equity found the property right either in the trademark or the trade name. If the plaintiff sued the defendant for invasion of the right of privacy be-

cause the defendant was about to publish some
private letters belonging to the plaintiff, equity
found the property right in the letters themselves.
Today, as a general rule, the requirement to establish the property right has been abandoned by the
majority of the equity courts and in some states this
has been accomplished by statute. Today, for example, if the plaintiff receives obscene phone calls
which invade his right of privacy, where is the
property interest to be protected? There isn't any.
Because of this, can the plaintiff obtain relief? He
can, even though only personal rights to be free of
such calls are involved. Today, most enlightened
writers want the basis for jurisdiction to be personal rather than property and equity courts are no
longer pretending that property rights are involved
nor are they creating legal fictions to obtain that
same result.

e. *Should the Hardships be Balanced?*

Next to the question of whether or not the plaintiff has an adequate remedy at law, the question of
balancing the hardships is perhaps the most important in making the determination as to whether or
not the injunction should issue. What equity actually does is to weigh the hardship to the plaintiff if
the injunction is denied against the hardship to the
defendant if it is granted. In such situations, there
are two views. One is the minority view holding
that the hardships should not be balanced at all
where the plaintiff has been injured substantially by
some wrongful act of the defendant. For example,

if you have an encroachment problem which is innocent and hardship to the defendant outweighs the
benefit of the injunction to the plaintiff, under the
majority view the injunction would not be granted
and the plaintiff would be awarded damages. Under the minority view, the plaintiff would be granted the injunction and the defendant would have to
tear down the encroachment. In the majority view,
the hardship of tearing down the building out-
weighs the injunction, so the plaintiff receives damages for the encroachment. There is one situation,
however, on which all courts seem to agree, and
that is if the defendant's acts are wilful and intentional, the injunction is granted regardless of the
hardship on the defendant. For example, if he built
the encroachment intentionally, knowing that it was
on the plaintiff's property and in total disregard of
any efforts by the plaintiff to discourage him. Or,
if there is a continuing nuisance which the defendant realizes is obnoxious and is interfering with the
quiet enjoyment of the land by the plaintiff, the
courts will characterize such a continuing nuisance
as wilful and intentional.

What factors are considered by the court which
follow the majority view to balance the hardships
between the parties? As indicated above, the first
such factor would be to see if the conduct by the
defendant is wilful. If so, there will be no balancing. What are the relative uses of the property?
What is the cost of removal as compared to the
value of the land? For example, if to remove the
encroachment is a costly one whereas the land on
which it sits is cheap, the decision will usually be for

the defendant. Is the public interest involved?
Suppose a factory is in a small town which would
have to shut down if the factory is removed? Here
the courts would consider the economic impact involved and if the public interest would be injured to
a greater extent, the injunction would not be issued
even if the harm is caused by wilful violations of the
defendant. In many such instances, however, the
court issues a limited injunction to give the defendant time to see if he can minimize, abate, or even
eliminate the interference with the property of the
plaintiff. These are applicable particularly with respect to nuisances. Everyone recognizes that there
is a certain amount of normal interference with the
use of property. When that interference becomes
unreasonable, the wrongdoer should be ordered to
correct the situation or pay for it. One factor in
this regard is to examine the conduct of the parties
and see if the nuisance existed at the time the
plaintiff occupied the property. If so, this factor
alone will be weighed heavily against him.

f. What are the Defenses to Injunctions?

The two major defenses are those of laches and
unclean hands. Laches, which is the passage of an
unreasonable period of time having a prejudicial
effect on the defendant, is more commonly used in
injunctions whereas the defense of unclean hands
appears most frequently in the unfair competition
cases. Where the defense of unclean hands is involved, it must pertain to the matter in issue rather
than to the general conduct of the plaintiff. Both
of these defenses have been treated in detail in

other sections of this book. Those details apply equally to the defenses to injunctions.

Freedom of speech can be used as a defense in defamation and libel cases. In such matters, the doctrine of "prior restraint" is involved, and equity hesitates to issue injunctions against slander and libel for this reason. In such cases, the remedy at law is adequate and the plaintiff will collect damages. If the libel is in the area of commercial disparagement or trade libel, equity will interfere with an injunction in order to protect the property right involved. For example, equity can enjoin a publication which creates unfair competition. There is no problem as long as competitors compare their products and even say "mine is best." This is known as a conditional privilege and there is no problem as long as the language remains general.

If the defendant receives an injunction to remove an encroachment from the land of the plaintiff, it is quite obvious that he must enter upon the plaintiff's land to do so. If the plaintiff refuses to let him trespass on the land for this purpose, the defendant can use this refusal as a defense to the injunction.

Courts of equity will not ordinarily enjoin the commission of a crime particularly where the government is a plaintiff. But the mere fact that the act constituting a nuisance is also a crime does not hinder the use of the civil processes to procure its abatement where the use of property is a part. For example, in civil rights cases, is the remedy adequate where the defendant is fined in the criminal action for every black person not admitted to his store? Will this remedy get the black into the store? It is for this reason that the remedy is inadequate and equity will issue an injunction and may put the defendant in jail for civil contempt if he does not comply. But doesn't this deny him his right to a jury trial? Has he been convicted beyond a reasonable doubt? What about the presumption of innocence? Isn't this dual punishment? Equity says we are not punishing the defendant but protecting the plaintiff so no constitutional issue is involved.

If the problem is that of encroachment, both damages and ejectment should be discussed. These are inadequate if the encroachment is continuous or the sheriff refuses to eject.

If the problem involves a civil rights statute as where State X has a statute with a public rights section and the plaintiff, a black, is excluded from it, and such violations are classified as a misdemeanor only, can the plaintiff get an injunction? If the statute does not state that injunctive relief is available, determine if it was the legislative intent to provide it. In such situations, the multiplicity of suits would be the basis for issuing the injunction because the criminal sanction would not be adequate. If the statute provided for a $50 fine for violations, will this get the black into public places to eat? Also look at the feasibility arguments. How can the court supervise such an injunction? What is the restaurant owner actually doing wrong? Where is the property right to be protected? Civil rights are equally as important as property rights.

It is true that equity will not enjoin a crime and the offense here does not fit into a tort. It is established only by statute which calls for criminal penalties. However, it is an axiom of law that no man shall be denied a remedy if he is wronged. Modern courts would tend to let the plaintiff in the restaurant and relief should not be denied simply because a criminal sanction exists.

IV. DAMAGES

1. INTRODUCTION

The purpose of this chapter is to discuss the broad field of Compensatory Damages which concerns itself with recovering "losses" of the injured party. It is designed to provide the student with a succinct understanding of the principles of Compensatory Damages so that those principles may be applied to specific situations. Particular attention should be paid to the subject of Damages. There is a tendency to de-emphasize it in favor of equity and its remedies; however, once the student comprehends the real importance and position of Damages within the system of remedies, he will realize that in just about every factual situation he should always consider the subject of Damages. The first reason is the most obvious one. If the remedy in damages at law is adequate, there is no point in even considering the equitable remedies. On the other hand, if they are not adequate at law and the equitable actions predominate, the plaintiff can receive both his equitable relief and damages as well. Thus, Damages, as a subject can cut across both law and equity with one additional convenience. The basic rules concerning the award of Damages do not change because they are awarded in equity rather than in law. Thus, the knowledge of the subject can serve the purposes of both law and equity.

2. COMPENSATORY DAMAGES

As indicated earlier, the fundamental purpose of compensatory damages is to make the plaintiff whole by compensating him for actual losses where a tort is involved or for his lost expectancies if the relationship was a consensual one. The form which these damages take is that of "money" which is considered to be a substitute for what the plaintiff has lost or suffered. If there is still a chance that the plaintiff can get back the very thing which he wants, the recovery would then be "in specie" rather than substitutionary. The student should not get the impression, however, that every award of a money judgment is also compensatory in nature. For example, nominal damages in the form of money can be awarded to protect a right of the plaintiff even though no actual harm has occurred. Or, punitive damages can be imposed upon the defendant in order to deter or punish him rather than to compensate the plaintiff.

As a standard rule, the student should examine the losses of the plaintiff first. Relying upon the theory that damages are intended to make the plaintiff whole, it is only logical to see immediately just what the plaintiff has lost and whether or not giving him compensation for those losses would be adequate. Making this determination early will frequently furnish one with a basis for equity jurisdiction. As discussed in Chapter III, the broad base for determining whether or not the case will be heard in equity is: IS THE REMEDY AT LAW ADEQUATE? Through case law, certain specific instances have arisen in which the remedy at law has been determined to be inadequate; cases involving the sale of land because land is considered to be unique, cases involving unique chattels such as priceless art collections and treasures, cases where a fiduciary relationship exists and it has been breached, multiplicity of suits brought about through a continuing tort, and situations where the damages are too speculative and where a far superior remedy, such as bill of accounting or reformation, is available only in equity. These can be used as guidelines for determining the availability of equity jurisdiction and where they are present it can be determined very quickly that the remedy at law is inadequate. Thus the student can use one of two approaches, i.e., determine just what damages the plaintiff is entitled to at law and if these will restore him to the position he would have been in had the tort not occurred or the contract not been breached, then the remedy at law may be adequate. On the other hand, the student can apply the above guidelines to his fact situation and, if any one fits, the remedy at law will be inadequate. In any event, one must gain admittance to equity's door before he can avail himself of equity's remedies and the key to that door is the inadequacy of the remedy at law in a given situation

3. TYPES OF DAMAGES

There are two types or categories of damages: "General" and "Special" (also referred to as "consequential"). In treating these, the courts proceed first with the general and then follow with the special. Actually, the courts do not favor the special and, as will be seen, they surround them with certain limitations which, depending upon the action, may eliminate the recovery entirely. Thus, it is necessary to place the major emphasis on the recovery of the general damages. It can be accepted as a natural rule that once the injury has been established, the courts will grant the appropriate remedy; however, as has been, and will be, established, the courts are not interested in making a millionaire of the plaintiff. Rather, they are concerned that he should be put in the position he would have been in had the tort not occurred or the contract been carried out. This objective can be accomplished ordinarily through general damages and the student or young attorney should concentrate on this area before proceeding to that of special damages.

a. General Damages

General damages are those which will usually "flow" in the case of a tort from the wrong itself or, in the case of a contract, from its breach. It is for this reason that these damages do not have to be pleaded specially. They "arise" naturally and logically from either the tort or the breach of the contract.

The basic rule governing the recovery of general damages in tort actions is that foreseeability is not a limitation on such recovery. While it is recognized that in the tort of negligence, for example, foreseeability of some harm is necessary to establish that tort, once it has been established, the tortfeasor cannot claim that at the time of the tort he did not have any reason to foresee all of the injuries which did occur. Substantive tort law supports this approach by cautioning that the tortfeasor takes the victim "as he finds him".

The general rule regarding breaches of contracts, whether real or personal property is involved, is that the injured party shall recover that compensation which will leave him as well off as he would have been had the contract been fully performed. The general intention of the law giving damages in an action for the breach of a contract is to put the injured party, so far as it can be done by money, in the same position as he would have been had the contract been carried out. It is not the policy of the law to put a plaintiff in a better position than if the defendant had carried out his contract. For this purpose, compensatory damages are measured generally in terms of "loss of expectancy" or "loss of bargain". Compensation in this context, therefore, is the value of the performance of the contract and the main purpose behind the term "value" is an economic one. Courts support this by using such terms as "intrinsic value", or "value to the owner." In such cases, where the general damages are based upon value, the plaintiff can prove these through expert testimony, market reports, comparable sales, showing the income that the property might produce in the future (capitalization of income), or even the opinion of the owner himself as to its value. However, even in using the "value" approach, the courts are guided by the basic goal of damages to restore, as much as possible, the plaintiff to his original position. Where this will not occur, the courts are becoming more liberal in the use of special damages to assist in achieving that goal. In other instances, courts are not hesitant to substitute a measure different than value in order to make the plaintiff whole, such as replacement or repair cost.

An added element of concern with respect to damages is that they must be established with certainty to avoid being challenged as pure speculation or conjecture. This is one element, however, to which the word "reasonable" can be applied as long as there is sufficient proof that damages do, in fact, exist. Once this is established, the court can apply a reasonable person test to determine the probable loss of the plaintiff. This requirement is critical where loss of profits is involved; however, one should look for an experience factor to aid in its solution.

b. Special Damages

Once the general damages are settled, the court then looks at the special damages. These are injuries or losses which must be pleaded specially and are subject to certain limitations. They cannot be too remote from the injury; there must be a causal relation ("but for" rule) between the injury and the damages; and, they must be proven with a reasonable degree of certainty. It should be quite obvious, therefore, that the decision to plead special damages as compared with general damages, is circumscribed rather rigidly by the courts. This alone should alert the student to the fact that special damages are not favored by the courts. This should further alert the student to the fact that the area of special damages should be approached only after an exhaustive effort has been made to insure that all possible damages recoverable from the injury or breach have been included in the general damages. There is one specific guideline which can be followed in this respect: the object of damages is to make the plaintiff whole—it is not to make him rich at the expense of the defendant.

The requirement of causation seems to be a rather obvious one. If the plaintiff has suffered no loss, or would have suffered the same loss without the defendant's wrong, then the plaintiff cannot recover. His special damages, therefore, must have been caused in fact by the defendant, and the wrong must be the proximate cause of the damage suffered. Once this has been established, the wrongdoer in a tort action is charged with all injuries which naturally flow therefrom even though they were not foreseen at the time of the misconduct. In contract cases, while the term "proximate cause" is not used, the effect is still the same by claiming that special damages must be "within the contemplation of the parties at the time they made their contract," otherwise there can be no recovery. This amounts to an additional requirement known as "foreseeability." The origin of this rule is found in the landmark case of Hadley v. Baxendale (156 Eng.Rep. 145) decided in 1854. In that case, a mill had stopped production because of a broken shaft.

The miller sent the shaft by carrier to an engineer to make a new one from the old pattern. The carrier was told that "the mill was stopped and that the shaft must be sent immediately." The carrier promised to get it to the engineer in a day but there was an undue delay which caused the mill to be out of operation for several days longer. The miller sued the carrier for his loss of profits for that period of time but the Court of Exchequer held that these losses could not be recovered because they were not "foreseeable." The court held that special damages were not recoverable except in two situations. First, if they could reasonably be considered as arising naturally from the breach and second, if they were "in the contemplation of the parties at the time they made the contract, as the probable result of the breach of it." The first rule is the standard measure used to recover general damages while the second is that used for the recovery of special damages. Thus, "foreseeability" is a further limitation on the recovery of special damages. Some courts have narrowed this even further by holding that one was not liable for special damages unless he agreed, at least tacitly, to assume the risk of these particular damages. This is known as the Tacit Agreement Rule which has been rejected as far as the sale of goods is concerned by the Uniform Commercial Code.

There is much controversy over the Hadley rule stemming from the application of the rule to the Hadley case itself. As the facts of the case indicate "the carrier was told that the mill was stopped and that the shaft must be sent immediately." This understanding occurred at the time of the making of the agreement. Since the mill was already stopped and the carrier promised to get the shaft to the engineer in one day, it is difficult to rationalize that any delay in such delivery would not result in a corresponding delay in the opening of the mill and that this particular situation "was not in the contemplation of the parties" at the time they made the agreement. It appears that they not only contemplated it but that the carrier tacitly assumed the risk that such would occur if there was any delay in delivering the shaft. Nevertheless, such controversies are what law review articles are made of and will be left to that medium for further exploration.

Once the plaintiff proves the causation in fact plus the non-remoteness of the damage, he is required to prove the amount of his special losses with reasonable certainty. Stated another way, the courts do not award speculative damages. On the other hand, the plaintiff is not required to be mathematically precise in making this determination. For example, the problem is far more aggravated in tort cases than in those involving contracts. How do you measure the damages caused by the intentional infliction of mental distress? What is the economic value of libel or slander? In contract actions on the other hand, mental distress is not an element for special damages and the economic value of a breach can be established by examining the contract price and the market price at the time of the breach. The general rule is that the courts expect the plaintiff to produce the best evidence he can concerning his special damages. He has a particular problem if he is trying to recover lost profits from a new business venture. If it is an established business, the court can find a basis for arriving at such a figure; however, if it is a new venture, the courts will hold the damages are too speculative for recovery.

The U.C.C. in §§ 2–709, 2–710, and 2–715, provides certain situations in which "incidental" or "consequential" damages are awarded. For example, section 2–710 states that "Incidental damages to an aggrieved seller include any commercially reasonable charges, expenses or commissions incurred in stopping delivery, in the transportation, care and custody of goods after the buyer's breach, in connection with return or resale of the goods or otherwise resulting from the breach." Section 2–715 provides as another example that "Incidental damages resulting from the seller's breach include expenses reasonably incurred in inspection, receipt, transportation and care and custody of goods rightfully rejected, any commercially reasonable charges, expenses or commissions in connection with effective cover and any other reasonable expense incident to the delay or other breach." Under subsection (2) of § 2–715, it is significant to note that consequential damages may be recovered for "injury to person or property proximately resulting from any breach of warranty."

c. *Punitive Damages*

Punitive damages are imposed to punish or deter and are awarded because the defendant has acted in a manner which exceeds the normal standards of decent conduct between individuals. They are discretionary and are never given as a matter of right and are left to the determination of the jury. In making its determination, the jury considers whether or not the conduct of the defendant has been malicious, reckless, oppressive, abusive, evil, wicked, or so gross that some type of deterrent punishment is necessary. The deterrent punishment usually takes the form of money. In this respect, punitive damages are also referred to as "vindictive" or "exemplary" or as "smart money." It should be apparent that in considering punitive damages, the examination should begin with the defendant's conduct from which one can assess his state of mind. The problem is akin to that of finding intent in contract actions which is manifested by the defendant through his exterior conduct. Speaking of contracts, it is frequently stated that punitive damages cannot be recovered in a breach of contract suit; however, the mind of the defendant may be just as evil in a breach of contract as it is in a tort. Nevertheless, the majority rule denies the recovery of punitive damages in breach of contract situations.

There is one rule which is rather standard with respect to punitive damages and that is they may not be recovered unless the plaintiff has suffered some actual loss or damage. This should flow from the bad faith, malice, abuse or evil with which the defendant influences his conduct. It is difficult to envision a situation without loss or damage where the defendant is influenced by such malicious motives. It is only human nature that such motives will not be satisfied without some form of corresponding injury to the object of that influence. Nevertheless, such reasoning will not satisfy the courts—actual damages must exist before the jury can award punitive damages. Once these actual damages have been established, some jurisdictions take the position that the punitive damages must bear some relation to the compensatory damages received. The relationship goes so far as to treat the compensatory damages as a ceiling for the punitive damages. It is difficult to rationalize this if the standard for the award of punitive damages is the mental culpability of the defendant. Compensatory damages are supposed to compensate the plaintiff for all the injury done to either his person or his property, including those for mental suffering and anguish. Once these have been established and resolved, consideration then turns to the award of punitive damages. Why shouldn't the plaintiff next be compensated for the degree of malice or ill will under which the tort occurred? And, if the jury finds that such bad faith is outrageous, why should their award be limited to that of the compensatory damages? One school of thought would reject punitive damages entirely which are described as either criminal or quasi-criminal for which there is no place in a purely civil action whose object is to restore the plaintiff to the position he would have been in had the tort not occurred or the contract not been breached. Once this has been accomplished, hasn't the plaintiff received all to which he has been entitled? The only answer is, of course, that the award of punitive damages is intended to have a deterring effect within society itself. The courts are interested more than any other agency in limiting litigation. One of the ways is to "exemplify" a situation which can serve as an object lesson to others in a similar situation. Unfortunately, the question of whether or not they are intended to produce a deterring effect has been clouded by the fact that large punitive damage awards are given by juries to pay the expenses of the plaintiff in prosecuting the lawsuit. Isn't this really a fraud on the jury itself? Are the plaintiff's expenses a proper measure of punitive damages? The answer is clearly in the negative and one will be hard put to find support in the court's instructions to the jury concerning punitive damages.

There appears to be many contradictions in the award of punitive damages. For example, it is frequently stated that they cannot be recovered in a breach of contract suit and this is the general rule. However, the mind of the defendant may be just as evil in a breach of contract suit as in a tort. Another standard rule is that equity will not grant punitive damages on the grounds that they are quasi-criminal in nature. It is difficult, however, to reconcile this with the criminal contempt proceedings of a court of equity which will incarcerate an individual for up to six months for his refusal to obey a decree of equity. Surely, such imprisonment is also quasi-criminal in nature since its object is to punish the individual for his failure to obey an order of the court of equity. There is, however, a minority rule that punitive damages may be recovered in a court of equity. There is also a third contradiction in the decisions concerning punitive damages. Jurisdictions will allow the jury to consider the financial condition of the defendant in making an award of punitive damages whereas they will not allow the same reasoning with respect to actual damages. Why the difference? Perhaps the answer is found in the intention of the courts to make such awards for the protection of society. Apparently, the soaking of one who can afford it will deter others who also can afford it from repeating the same type of outrageous misconduct. But isn't this actually begging the question? If they can really afford it, does it deter them or does it deter those who can't afford it? Probably the latter.

Finally, the student should be aware of other holdings with respect to the recovery of punitive damages. Some jurisdictions hold that unless the plaintiff recovers some compensatory damages, he cannot also recover punitive damages. This appears to be a step which precedes the previous discussion on the limitation of the amount of recovery of punitive damages to those of the compensatory damages. As indicated above, equity will not award punitive damages and, as a general rule, punitive damages are not awarded in breach of contract cases. And finally, a principal is not vicariously liable for the culpable torts of his agents.

d. Nominal Damages

At the opposite end of compensatory damages and punitive damages, one will find nominal damages. These are awarded in certain cases where there is no specific harm and only the establishment of a right is involved. In other words, as a general rule, actual damages need not be shown to receive nominal damages. On the other hand it is difficult to find case law where the plaintiff began by seeking nominal damages. Rather, they are awarded after the court rejects the plea of the plaintiff that compensatory damages should be awarded. This does not mean that the plaintiff will be awarded nominal damages in every instance where he does not collect compensatory damages. There are certain causes of action which require proof of actual injury such as fraud. Where this is required but not proven, not even nominal damages will be awarded.

e. *Interest*

The award of interest is governed generally by state statutes. There are two types which may be awarded: Pre-judgment and Post-judgment. Pre-judgment is measured generally from the time the claim was due until judgment is entered. Post-judgment, which is the more favored of the two, is awarded from the time the judgment is entered.

The basic theory behind awarding interest is to give the plaintiff what he probably would have obtained if he invested his money during the time that he was actually deprived of it. This means that the legal interest rate at that time is used as a measure of damages. If the damages cannot be determined with any reasonable degree of market certainty, interest, usually of the Pre-judgment

type, may not be awarded. The Restatement of Torts
in Section 913 allows interest in certain situations
unless the plaintiff elects restitution as his recovery. He can get it where land, chattels, or other
objects have been taken, detained, or destroyed
where their value can be determined from market
prices between the time of the taking to the time of
trial. As a general rule, interest is not granted on
any amount given for bodily harm, emotional distress, or for injury to reputation. He can also get
interest under the Restatement "for other harm to
pecuniary interests from the time of the accrual of
the cause of action to the time of trial if the
payment of interest is required to avoid an injustice."

f. Attorney's Fees

Unless provided for by either contract or statute,
there is no blanket authority for the recovery of
attorney's fees. There are, of course, certain exceptions to this general rule, the most common being
that of a shareholder's derivative suit in which the
plaintiff, when he wins, can get reimbursement from
the corporation for attorney's fees. Another is in
equity in a civil contempt action where the fine may
include an award of attorney's fees. At the federal
level, it has long been a majority rule that counsel
fees may be awarded where the defense has been
maintained in bad faith. Care should be exercised
where the contract provides for the payment of
attorney's fees to only one of the parties. In many
states, these provisions are considered to be valid;

however, other states interpret such provisions to mean that the award is to be given to the party who prevails in the contract action. Finally, prevailing parties often get attorney's fees in actions under various federal Civil Rights Statutes.

4. SPECIAL RULES AFFECTING RECOVERY OF DAMAGES

There have been certain rules developed over the centuries which affect the amount of compensatory damages one might expect to recover. It cannot be assumed that just because the plaintiff prays compensation for certain losses that he will automatically get them. Rather, the recovery may well be limited either to certain rules which the courts will apply or actually to certain agreements made by the parties themselves. Examples of the former are the Avoidable Consequences Rule and the Collateral Source Rule and, the standard example of the latter is the Liquidated Damages provision in contract actions.

a. *Avoidable Consequences Rule*

Put in a negative way, this rule says that the plaintiff cannot recover any special damages which he could have avoided by reasonable acts or expenditures. Put affirmatively, it authorizes the recovery of such expenditures which the plaintiff makes reasonably to avoid or minimize the special damages caused by the defendant's misconduct. The theory behind the rule is that of economic waste and the defendant has the burden of proving that the plaintiff should have minimized. If both he and the plaintiff have equal opportunities to minimize, the defendant cannot complain if the plaintiff doesn't move first.

The avoidable consequences rule applies to both tort and contract actions. In both areas, the plaintiff must do all that he can but only from a reasonable standpoint to make the damages to the defendant as light as possible. If the expense to the plaintiff is out of proportion to the damages themselves, the plaintiff is not required to make any such unreasonable expenditures. In this connection, the use of this rule in examinations questions should be noted. It is more or less in the nature of a "trap" issue. Students concentrate so heavily on the substantive area that they overlook the avoidable consequences rule. The issue may arise by the simple but subtle reference to the fact that the plaintiff has been made aware of the situation by the defendant who seeks his help in a reasonable manner. If the plaintiff ignores the request on the basis that the parties have a contract and that the problem belongs squarely to the defendant under that contract, the plaintiff may later be haunted by the avoidable consequences rule if he could have taken reasonable actions to minimize the damages caused by the defendant and failed to do so.

b. *Collateral Source Rule*

Unlike the avoidable consequences rule which may work to the detriment of the plaintiff, the collateral source rule may work to his benefit provided that the plaintiff receives benefits from a source collateral to the defendant in either a tort or contract situation. If this is the situation, the defendant cannot use these to reduce his own liability in damages. There is one major exception to this rule which applies if the benefit is derived from the defendant himself. For example, if the defendant's insurance company pays the plaintiff's medical bills, these can be deducted from the defendant's liability to the plaintiff. If they are paid by the plaintiff's insurance company, however, they are considered to be from a collateral source which the defendant cannot claim. However, the rule concerning collateral payments is not confined to insurance matters alone. For example, an employee may recover damages for personal injuries although he has received wages from his employer during the period of his illness. Or, an injured party may claim medical services as damages even though they have been provided free-of-charge to him or have been paid for by his relatives. In other words, the defendant should not be credited for any money which the plaintiff receives from other sources. The reason for this is obvious. The tortfeasor should not be allowed to escape from his pecuniary liability merely because his victim has received benefit from a third party. If it were otherwise, the defendant would be receiving a windfall.

c. *Liquidated Damages*

Contracting parties can agree on a method for determining damages in the event of a breach. This is done usually where the damages themselves are very difficult to determine and the amount agreed upon is a reasonable forecast of just what the damages will be. In other words, where the forecast is difficult as to the amount of damages to be paid in the case of a breach, the agreement to pay a stipulated amount is known as liquidated damages. They are generally valid even though the plaintiff may get either more or less from the breached duty provided they are not considered by the courts to be in the nature of a penalty. If they are considered by the courts to be penal in nature, they will not be upheld. If, for example, the amount agreed upon is unreasonably and grossly disproportionate to the actual losses, the stipulated amount may be construed as a penalty. The difficulty in this respect lies in the clause which provides that it is the "sole" or "only" remedy for the breach. If this is the case the other party can rarely, if ever, get specific performance of the contract. The reason is an obvious one. Where the agreement contains express language between the parties, the courts cannot construe any different meaning to the language and are bound to uphold the language used. However, most contracts containing liquidated damages are not of the exclusive variety so that the courts tend to look upon the language as optional, i.e., giving the non-breaching party the right to claim either specific performance or the enforcement of the liquidated damages provision.

In order to justify an agreement containing liquidated damages, the damage which is to be expected if there is a breach must be either uncertain as to the amount or at least very difficult to prove. In addition, that amount must be reasonable in that it was not grossly disproportionate to the amount of the damages which the parties assumed it would be looking forward from the time that they made the agreement; in other words, using the foreseeability test of the rule of Hadley v. Baxendale. Finally, even if a liquidated damages provision is contained in the agreement, it will not be enforced where damage does not actually occur. This is indicated further in Restatement I, Contracts, § 339, which provides that "If the parties honestly but mistakenly suppose that a breach will cause harm that will be incapable or very difficult of accurate estimation, when in fact the breach causes no harm at all or none that is incapable of accurate estimation without difficulty, this advance agreement fixing the amount to be paid as damages for the breach . . . is not enforceable." In the ordinary contract, the court enforces the damages from the evidence offered. On the other hand, there is implied within a liquidated damages provision the understanding that the sum agreed upon will be within the fair range of the damages which the parties would be called upon to prove. So, if the damages never occur, the basis for their agreement would disappear and to enforce it would really amount to an extreme penalty.

Whenever the contract contains a liquidated damages provision, the question arises quite naturally as to whether or not specific performance of the contract will be granted. The majority rule is that specific performance will be granted where the money mentioned is intended to be only a security for the performance of the principal obligations. If, however, the money can be substituted for the performance of the act called for at the election of the one by whom the money is to be paid, equity will deny specific performance and leave the injured party to his remedy at law. Therefore, the liquidated damages clause will not in and of itself be a bar to the remedy of specific performance unless the language is so explicit as to call for the payment of liquidated damages as the "sole" or "only" remedy.

V. RESTITUTION

1. INTRODUCTION

Restitution is similar to compensatory damages as a remedy in that it may be substitutionary i.e., the restoration of money rather than specific property; or, "in specie" which would be the return of something which belongs to the plaintiff and is being held by the defendant. The emphasis between the two, however, is markedly different. Compensatory damages are based upon the losses of the plaintiff. Restitution, on the other hand, is based upon the gains of the defendant which it would be unjust for him to retain. In other words, he would be unjustly enriched. The law, therefore, forces him to disgorge those gains. This is supported by the Restatement of Restitution which provides on page 595 that "Actions for restitution have for their primary purpose taking from the defendant and restoring to the plaintiff something to which the plaintiff is entitled, or if this is not done, causing the defendant to pay the plaintiff an amount which will restore the plaintiff to the position he was before the defendant received the benefit." The remedy is, therefore, in accord with the over-all objective of remedies which is to place the plaintiff in the position he would have been in had the breach or the tort not occurred.

Restitution is not a punitive remedy; however, its measure of damages may well be determined by the tortiousness of the defendant's conduct in creating the situation which calls for restitution. Again, the Restatement of Restitution on page 556 provides the answer: "If the defendant was tortious in his acquisition of the benefit he is required to pay for what the other has lost although that is more than the recipient benefited. If he was consciously tortious in acquiring the benefit, he is also deprived of any profit derived from his subsequent dealing with it. If he was no more at fault than the claimant, he is not required to pay for losses in excess of benefit received by him and he is permitted to retain gains which result from his dealing with the property." At the outset, therefore, it is extremely important to examine first the losses of the plaintiff and then see whether or not the defendant has made any gains from the situation which he has created. If so, consideration should be given immediately to examining the conduct of the defendant in creating that situation. If it was done in bad faith, or as the result of fraud, or as the breach of a fiduciary duty, the defendant will be required to disgorge all of his profits without any consideration of apportioning any part of it to other than his tortious conduct. Once this determination has been made, reference should then be made to the equitable remedies which have been developed to reach the same result. These are: the constructive trust, accounting, the equitable lien, and subrogation, all of which will be discussed in detail in this chapter.

2. HISTORY OF RESTITUTION AT LAW

The student of law cannot understand the present procedures for restitution without knowing at least something about certain common law writs which were themselves restitutionary. For example, if the defendant was wrongfully in possession of the plaintiff's land and the plaintiff wanted his land returned to him, he would ask for ejectment which developed from the common law Writ of Trespass. Ejectment had as its objective the restoration of land to the plaintiff; however, since the plaintiff was not in possession but the defendant was, the question of legal title became an important issue in the case. The action of ejectment today provides the same basic remedy and creates the same problem with respect to title.

Both detinue and replevin were also restitutionary actions in the common law. Detinue was a form of action which was used for the recovery in specie of personal chattels from one who acquired them lawfully but retained them wrongfully, together with damages for the detention. Originally, the remedy was founded upon the delivery of goods to a bailee who later refused to redeliver them to the bailor. The gist of the action was the wrongful detainer by the bailee. Today, the action of detinue is proper in every case where the owner prefers to recover the specific property rather than damages for its conversion and no regard is had to the manner in which the defendant acquired possession. Replevin, on the other hand, was a personal action brought to recover the possession of goods unlawfully taken and unlawfully detained by another. In the original action the goods were redelivered to the original possessor on his pledging or giving security to prosecute an action for the purpose of trying the legality of the detention. In detinue, therefore, the defendant was given the option of returning the goods or of paying their value to the plaintiff. In replevin, the plaintiff could post a bond and recover his property immediately without waiting for a favorable judgment. Today, and this will be discussed in detail later in this chapter, if the defendant also claims a property interest in the goods, he can offer a counterbond and keep the property until final judgment.

It was the common law Writ of Assumpsit, however, which had the greatest impact on restitution because it did not involve either title or possession as did the writs for detinue and replevin. The actual predecessor for assumpsit was the action known as Debt which was the common law action to recover a certain specific amount of money or a sum that could readily be reduced to a certainty. Thus, even the Writ of Debt had as its objective a restitutionary goal at least from a substitutionary standpoint, in that the plaintiff was trying to get back money he had loaned to the defendant. However, none of these actions were based upon simple contracts as we know them today. The only contract action at that time was that of Covenant with its formal seal. Assumpsit developed from the theory that the defendant "undertook" to do something and he did it badly. For example, if he owed money to the plaintiff, he undertook a promise to pay it back. This approach was validated in the landmark Slade's Case (76 Eng.Rep. 1072) in which it was held that the plaintiff could bring his action in "indebitatus assumpsit" rather than debt. Thus the action could be brought on a simple, express contract. It was a form of action in which the debt was alleged to be due from the defendant in consideration of which the defendant had promised to pay it. It was merely a matter of time before the application was also made to implied in fact contracts and finally in quasi-contracts in the landmark case of Moses v. MacFerlan (97 Eng.Rep. 676) in 1760, in which the court emphasized the unjust enrichment policy which is behind all restitutionary actions. As the action developed after that decision, certain "common counts" were established in the pleading forms. The six major counts were for "money had and received"; "money paid for the benefit of the defendant"; "goods sold and delivered"; "land occupied and used"; "work and labor performed (Quantum Meruit)"; and the "value of the product (Quantum Valebant)". An examination of any of these counts will establish the restitutionary nature of the recovery. For example, in the "money had and received" count, the defendant was definitely enriched by the money which he had received from the plaintiff and was not repaying. The same thing applied to "goods sold and delivered" to the defendant who had not yet paid for them. In the "quantum meruit" ("work and labor performed") count, the defendant was enriched either by an express, or implied in fact contract for work performed by the plaintiff for which he was never paid. Thus, the historical principle of restitution based upon the policy of unjust enrichment by the defendant was established.

Restitution at law, however, is normally a remedy which is imposed on a defendant through the use of the quasi-contract. As the student will recall from his Contracts course, this differs from both the express and the implied-in-fact contracts in which one can find an agreement between the parties. In the quasi-contract there is no such agreement. The court establishes the agreement itself in order to prevent unjust enrichment. As such, quasi-contracts are not really contracts at all. Rather, they are a mere fiction created by the courts to impose a given remedy. The law creates it regardless of the intent of the parties to assure a just and equitable result.

Before leaving the subject of assumpsit, a certain amount of discussion is necessary to explain a particular phrase which one hears repeatedly in this context: "waive the tort and sue in assumpsit." As a standard rule, whenever a tortfeasor wrongfully takes, uses, withholds or disposes of the property of another, the victim has an action for conversion; however, as a plaintiff, he also has the option of waiving that tort and suing in assumpsit to prevent the unjust enrichment of the defendant tortfeasor. For example, assume that the defendant made some considerable gains from either selling or investing the property. If the plaintiff sued in tort, he would recover the market value of the property at the time of the conversion. He would not reach the gains of the defendant through the tort action. By waiving the tort and suing in assumpsit on the common count that the defendant "had and received" money for the benefit of the plaintiff, the gains could then be reached. Care should be taken, however, to insure that the tort involved can be waived. As a majority rule, most torts can be waived and the suit brought in assumpsit with the proper common count provided that there is unjust enrichment and the common count used is the proper one. In addition, case law has established that certain torts, such as defamation, cannot be waived for the obvious reason that the defendant who makes the defamatory statement rarely obtains any unjust enrichment from it. The best approach to the problem is to examine the damages which are recoverable under the applicable tort. Then examine the damages which would be recovered in assumpsit using the applicable count. Assumpsit, therefore, has the effect of enabling the court to create a quasi-contract between the parties to prevent the unjust enrichment of the defendant at the expense of the plaintiff.

3. DEVELOPMENT OF RESTITUTION IN EQUITY

In the previous section, reference was made to the use of ejectment as a form of common law action which was designed to be a restitutionary remedy for the plaintiff out of possession of his land to regain it from the defendant who was in the possession of it. This action brought into issue the legal title to the property itself and even if the defendant had obtained that title fraudulently, he could not be ejected at the common law because he did hold title. The plaintiff's remedy, therefore, at law was not adequate for him to regain his proper-

ty. It was for this type of situation that the equity
courts acting in personam based upon right, justice
and good conscience, developed the remedy of the
constructive trust. This meant, rather briefly, that
equity could order the defendant to reconvey the
property to the plaintiff by calling the defendant a
constructive trustee who was holding the property
for the benefit of the plaintiff.

a. The Constructive Trust

The first thing that must be established is that
the constructive trust has no relation to the law of
trusts. It arises purely by a construction in equity
and is independent of any actual or presumed intent
of the parties. It differs from the resulting trust in
which there is always the implied intention of the
parties to create a trust. It is in effect a fraud
remedying device. Equity imposes it as a method
for preventing unjust enrichment on the part of the
defendant who is retaining something belonging to
the plaintiff. It is interpreted by equity to mean
that the defendant is holding something which belongs to the plaintiff in trust for the plaintiff. If
the court of equity finds that the defendant is
holding either money or property of the plaintiff
which was acquired by unjust, unconscionable or
unlawful means, it will raise a trust in favor of the
plaintiff. Thus, any transaction may be the basis
for creating a constructive trust where the defendant holds either funds or property which in equity
and good conscience should be possessed by the
plaintiff. Because it is imposed by a court of equity
it is similar to the quasi-contract which is imposed

by a court of law to accomplish the same objective i.e., prevention of unjust enrichment by the defendant. By the same token, it differs from the quasi-contract which usually results in the award of a money judgment to the plaintiff; whereas, in equity, the court can actually order the defendant as "trustee" to transfer the property to the plaintiff who is the "beneficiary of the trust."

The Restatement of Restitution, § 160 (1937) provides that "where a person holding title to property is subject to an equitable duty to convey it to another on the ground that he would be unjustly enriched if he were permitted to retain it, a constructive trust arises." And in the Restatement, Restitution, § 190 (1937), "Where a person in a fiduciary relation to another acquires property, and the acquisition or retention of the property is in violation of his duty as fiduciary, he holds it upon a constructive trust for the other." The Restatement, Restitution, § 194 (1937) provides that "A fiduciary who purchases from a third person for himself individually property which it is his duty to purchase for the beneficiary holds it upon a constructive trust for the beneficiary. A person who agrees with another to purchase property on behalf of the other and purchases the property for himself individually holds it upon a constructive trust for the other even though he is not under a duty to purchase the property for the other." And, finally, the Restatement, Restitution, § 201 (1937) states "Where a fiduciary in violation of his duty to the beneficiary acquires property through the use of confidential information, he holds the property so acquired upon a constructive trust for the beneficiary."

There are certain requirements which must be met before the constructive trust will be imposed. The first and obvious one is that the property must be identified as belonging to the plaintiff. Second, it must appear that the defendant actually has the title to the property rather than mere possession. Third, the plaintiff must be able to follow or trace his property into the product held by the defendant. The easiest example of this would be the obtaining of stocks from the plaintiff by mistake or fraud. These are property which can be identified as belonging to the plaintiff; the defendant in either selling them or investing them, can appear to hold title to them; and the plaintiff should be able to follow or trace his property into the gains received by the defendant either from the sale of the stocks or into dividends received from the investment. This would also be an excellent example of waiving the tort and suing in assumpsit. Finally, as with all other equitable actions, the plaintiff must show in most jurisdictions that his remedy at law is inadequate. This is done generally by showing the advantages of the constructive trust over restitution at law in which the recovery is usually monetary. In the constructive trust, the plaintiff is actually trying to recover his own property from the defendant. Thus, he would have a priority over all other creditors who would have to content themselves with obtaining a share of any other assets belonging to the defendant. This is, indeed, one of the major purposes of using specific restitution through the constructive trust particularly where the defendant is insolvent. Also by using the element of tracing, the plaintiff can follow his property into the product of the defendant and place the constructive trust upon it. Usually, this is done in those cases where the defendant in breach of his trust has disposed of the property so that he can no longer convey it to the beneficial owner. It is in such cases that equity will allow the beneficial owner to follow his property into the exchanged property and if that has increased in value, the beneficial owner will obtain that benefit.

The usual situations under which the constructive trust will be imposed are those wherein the defendant has acquired title to property of the plaintiff by mistake, duress, undue influence, or fraud. A further extension brings it into the field of fiduciary relations. There is a tendency to believe that fiduciary relationships are limited to those of a trustee and beneficiary, attorney and client, guardian and ward; whereas, the rule is a much broader one and encompasses any relationship in which confidence is given on one side to a dominating party on the other. If the property, however, is obtained by theft or conversion, equity will not impose a constructive trust upon it because the defendant never had the title to it. But, if he sells the stolen property and uses the money to buy another product, the plaintiff can have a constructive trust placed upon the product merely by tracing the stolen property into the money and thence into the new product. Looking at the remedies at law in such an instance, the plaintiff can sue in conversion and his judgment would be the value of the goods at the time and place of that conversion. Or, if the goods are still in the hands of the wrongdoer, an action in replevin would be a complete remedy. Even if the goods are sold, the tort of conversion can be waived and the suit brought in assumpsit on the count of "money had and received." As long as the goods can be identified either originally or through tracing action, the thief can be treated as a trustee either of the proceeds or of any property into which it has been transformed. This would be, of course, the use of the constructive trust. He may want to consider other equitable remedies such as accounting or the imposition of an equitable lien. With respect to the latter, however, the tracing requirement is still present and if the original property cannot be traced, the lien may not be granted.

b. The Equitable Lien

Assume, as was done above, that the defendant obtained certain funds from the plaintiff by fraud and used them to buy shares of stock. Clearly, the plaintiff has a claim against the defendant for the amount of the money fraudulently taken by the defendant. In such a circumstance, the court of equity can impose an equitable lien upon the stock which is a charge on it to secure the debt owed to the plaintiff. As with any other lien, it can be foreclosed, i.e., the property sold and the proceeds used to pay the amount of the debt. The equitable lien holder would have priority over all other unsecured creditors because the lien sets aside that property for the plaintiff. It should also be noted that the plaintiff could have used the constructive trust rather than the equitable lien if he wanted the stocks rather than just using them as security for the stolen money. A deciding factor in determining which to use would be whether or not the stocks have increased in value.

As with the constructive trust, there are certain requirements which must be met before the equitable lien will be imposed. The element of tracing is common to both actions. The plaintiff must trace his property to the defendant in such a manner as to show some obligation to pay for it. Second, it must be shown that the defendant has the title to the property which will be subjected to the lien. Third, the doctrine of prevention of unjust enrichment must apply. Most equitable liens arise today through the mutual agreement of the parties. The standard example is that of a borrower of money who agrees that certain property which he has will be security for the loan. Where such mutual agreement is not present, however, the equitable lien can be imposed particularly to prevent unjust enrichment. Finally, the major difference between the constructive trust and the equitable lien lies in the fact that the constructive trust gives a complete title to the property to the plaintiff whereas the equitable lien gives him only a security interest which can be foreclosed to satisfy the debt. In other words, the constructive trust is based upon the theory that the property must be that of the plaintiff and not the defendant whereas a lien views the property as belonging to the defendant but subject to a security interest by the plaintiff.

c. *Subrogation*

Subrogation is a remedial device which equity uses to prevent unjust enrichment. It was developed by equity because at the common law, whether a debt was paid by the primary obligor or by another secondarily liable, the debt was extinguished entirely and there could not be any subrogation of the creditor's rights or remedies on the original obligation. Equity held, and this is the majority rule in this country, that whenever a surety or guarantor pays the creditor's debt, the surety or guarantor is subrogated to all of the creditor's rights and remedies against the principal for its collection. Therefore, it is really the substitution of another person in the place of the creditor to give the surety or guarantor the benefit of any security that the creditor may hold against the principal debtor. As an example, assume that A owes B $500 with C as the surety for A on the debt. C pays B the $500 and the debt is discharged. C is subrogated to all of B's rights against A. The Restatement, Restitution, § 162 (1937) states "Where property of one person is used in discharging an obligation owed by another or a lien upon the property of another, under such circumstances that the other would be unjustly enriched by the retention of the benefit thus conferred, the former is entitled to be subrogated to the position of the obligee or lienholder."

Subrogation is not applied to a volunteer who pays the debt for the benefit of another without any assignment or agreement for subrogation. Subrogation is really a form of assignment in which the assignee is substituted to the rights of the paid-off creditor. It will be effectuated whenever (1) the one claiming it has in fact paid the debt; (2) that in doing so he was not a volunteer but had a direct interest in the discharge of the debt; (3) that he was secondarily liable for the debt usually as either a surety or guarantor; and (4) that no injustice would be done to the other party.

d. *Accounting for Profits*

This is an equitable remedy which is imposed on one who occupies a fiduciary relationship holding income producing trust property. He is under an obligation to produce the property and to account for any income received from it. Examples would be where he sells real estate or rents it. Today, it is also used in such actions as unfair competition, trademark infringement and copyright infringement to obtain an accounting of the profits made by the infringor. Thus, the fiduciary relationship is not essential in all cases and the court uses this action to determine exactly which of the profits is to be attributed to the wrong and which can be allocated to the efforts of the defendant irrespective of the wrong done to the plaintiff.

The action of Account began at the common law and was used initially to require bailiffs to account for their period of stewardship. It was not extensive, however, until equity began to use it by appointing auditors to examine accounts in greater depth. The situation in which it was most used by equity was where a fiduciary relationship existed and the trustee was required to account for the profits which he had received. Today, it is used by equity primarily in situations where a constructive trust has been imposed and it is necessary to determine which, if any, of the profits are due to his misconduct and which to his own labor and skill. Whenever this question arises, problems concerning expenses of production, fixed overhead, income tax and the offset of losses against profits must be considered. As a general rule, if the misconduct has been intentional, malicious and in bad faith, the courts have not hesitated to give all of the profits to the plaintiff. This is particularly true in the case of deducting income tax. Where this is not the case and despite the difficulty of ascertaining it, the defendant should try to establish just how much of the income tax can be attributed to the profits of the plaintiff and those from his own efforts. With respect to the expenses of production, he can deduct the costs of the materials and labor used in the manufacture of the item. Fixed overhead is generally denied because such personnel are generally being paid regardless of the new item. Why then should the tortfeasor be allowed to pro-rate their costs against the new item? There are situations also in which the defendant may realize savings within his own company as a result of the information which he appropriated from the plaintiff. The courts have considered these savings to be profits which can be proven from the books of the company itself.

e. *Rescission and Reformation*

Both rescission and reformation are restitutionary remedies in a narrowly defined context and both are discussed in detail in Chapters VI and VII.

4. MEASUREMENT CRITERIA FOR RESTITUTION

In the previous chapter on Damages, it was determined that the measure of damages which is used is that of "value" either in the form of "diminished value" or "replacement cost." Just what is the measured used for restitution? To answer this, one has to recall that the primary purpose for restitution is to take something from the defendant to which the plaintiff is entitled and restore it to the plaintiff. If this cannot be done, the defendant will be required to pay the plaintiff an amount which will put him in the position he was before the defendant received the benefit. The problem arises where the value of what was received and what was lost are different. There are certainly no problems where both values are equal. But there are situations in which the plaintiff loses more than the defendant gains and frequently the defendant gains more than the plaintiff has lost. In such cases, the measure of restitution is determined by examining the conduct of the defendant which created the situation for which the restitution is being sought. If his conduct was tortious, malicious, abusive, oppressive, or otherwise in bad faith, the defendant will be required to pay for what the plaintiff has lost even though it is more than he received and he will be deprived also of any profits he received from dealing with the plaintiff's property. If, on the other hand, he is no more to blame than the plaintiff, he will not be required to pay for losses in excess of the benefit which he received and he will be permitted to retain any gains which resulted from his own use of the property of the plaintiff.

If the defendant still has the property of the plaintiff who is interested in its actual return, the measurement would be "in specie" rather than substitutionary. Such a recovery depends generally upon either the legal title or an equitable interest in the property which is being held by the defendant. If, for example, the plaintiff has the legal title, he should have very little difficulty in recovering the res, unless, of course, it has been transferred to a bona fide purchaser for value. Where this has occurred, the recovery would have to be a substitutionary one. If the res was an ordinary chattel which has been disposed of by the defendant, the recovery would also be substitutionary and probably at law rather than in equity. If, however, the chattel is a unique one, the recovery would be in equity and would, at the option of the plaintiff, be "in specie". There is one distinction which should be clarified at this time. If money itself was the res taken by the defendant, its recovery would be in specie rather than substitutionary.

Another approach to the question of measurement is to examine the benefit actually received by the defendant particularly where money damages rather than a specific item is sought to be recovered. For example, assume that the plaintiff put a swimming pool in the back yard of the defendant without an agreement of any kind between the two. If he was a trespasser and was trying to force a sale of the pool on the defendant, even though the defendant received a benefit which can be measured, he will not be required to make any restitution because of the defense that the plaintiff is either a volunteer or an officious intermeddler. If the entry was made in good faith and mistakenly, and valuable improvements were made on the property, the common law rule is that the owner does not have to pay for these improvements. This common law rule has been changed by "betterment statutes" in many of the states which provide either for the removal of the improvement or an option to the owner to pay for the improvement or sell the land to the other party. While the court may use any one of these measures, the one used most frequently is that the plaintiff can expect to recover the amount by which his improvements have increased the land's value on the market. This would certainly be a proper application of measuring the benefit received by the defendant. There is one exception to this general rule and that occurs when the plaintiff puts improvements on the land of the defendant but they are destroyed before the defendant can make any use of them. If the plaintiff did this by mistake, the defendant cannot be expected to make any type of restitution; however, if the plaintiff was acting under an agreement with the defendant, he should at least get the reasonable value of his work and materials up to the time that the property was destroyed.

5. COMMINGLING OF FUNDS

The question of restitution becomes particularly sticky where the defendant has commingled the funds of the plaintiff with his own. The major difficulty arises because it is virtually impossible for the plaintiff to trace his own money into the fund and thence into a product or gains received by the defendant. For this reason, the common law rule was that no tracing resulted. Various theories have been advanced to solve this problem. One was the old English rule known as "first in first out", which has been discarded by most jurisdictions. Under that rule, if a wrongdoer deposited his own money into the account first, this would be considered as the first money withdrawn and what was left in the account would belong to the victim. If the victim's money was deposited first, this would be considered as the first money withdrawn. The effect of the rule is quite obvious. As long as the defendant deposited the funds first, whatever he withdrew would be considered as his own money and hence any product or profits he received from the expenditure would be his and could not be reached by the plaintiff. The rule was later reinforced by presuming that the money of the wrongdoer was withdrawn first from the commingled fund and that the amount remaining in the account belonged to the plaintiff. This is known as Hallet's Rule. Another possibility for tracing arose under the "Swollen Assets" rule which provided that when the wrongdoer put the victim's funds into his own account, his assets were considered to be "swollen" by the victim's money and subject to either a constructive trust or equitable lien. The modern approach, as contained in Section 211 of the Restatement of Restitution quoted below, is to allow an equitable lien for the full amount of the plaintiff's claim on both the funds traceable into property purchased by the wrongdoer and on those funds remaining in the account. The plaintiff, in some instances, is given an option, known as the "Option Rule" of using the constructive trust or the equitable lien either on the product of the commingled funds or on those funds remaining in the account. This "Option Rule" usually applies where the wrongdoer acts consciously. Also, if the wrongdoer depletes the fund and later restores it with the intent of restoring the victim's money, then the equitable lien will extend to the full amount of the account. Some courts say there is a presumed restitution of the victim's money in such a situation. Reference should be made, however, to local state statutes with respect to rules governing the commingling of funds.

The Restatement of Restitution, § 209 (1937) states "Where a person wrongfully mingles money of another with money of his own, the other is entitled to obtain reimbursement out of the fund." Section 210 continues "Where a person wrongfully mingles money of another with money of his own and with the mingled fund acquires property, the other is entitled to an equitable lien upon the property to secure his claim for reimbursement." Section 211 also provides that "Where a person wrongfully mingles money of another with money of his own and subsequently makes withdrawals from the mingled fund, the other is entitled to an equitable lien upon the part which remains and the part which is withdrawn or upon their product except as stated in Subsection (3). If the wrongdoer knew that he was acting wrongfully, the other is entitled at his option to a proportionate share both of the part which remains and of the part which is withdrawn or of their product, except as stated in Subsection (3)." Subsection (3) provides that "Where the wrongdoer has effectively separated the money of the other from his own money, the other is entitled to, and only to, his own money or its product."

6. DEFENSES

Restitution may be denied where there has been a changed position on the part of the defendant; where a bona fide purchaser for value is involved; because of a discharge for value; or because the plaintiff is a volunteer or officious intermeddler.

a. *Changed Position*

The Restatement, Restitution, Section 142 (1937) provides that "restitution can be denied or reduced if circumstances have changed after one receives a benefit and that change makes it inequitable to require restitution." The emphasis here is on the word "inequitable" in that equity balances the hardships between the parties provided, of course, that there is no bad faith or fraud on the part of the recipient of the benefit to begin with. In making this determination, equity examines whether or not the defendant actually received the benefit or did he pass it on to others? Second, in reliance on the benefit, just how far has the defendant changed his position? The majority of cases which denied restitution found that the recipient never received any benefit because he passed it on to others. Most involved situations in which overpayments were made and the recipient passed on the excess, for example, where the executor of an estate receives an overpayment from a debtor and then passes the money on to the heirs, or an agent who receives an overpayment and passes it on to his principal. In such cases, does the initial recipient have any net benefit which he should disgorge on the theory of unjust enrichment? No if he has acted in good faith and the majority rule does not require him to try to recover the overpayment and return it to the plaintiff. If, instead of passing the benefit on to others in good faith, the recipient uses it for his own personal living expenses, even that of supporting others, he cannot claim changed position as a defense. It is true that he no longer has the money. It may also be true that he has in effect "passed it on to others"; however, one cannot contest that he did receive a net benefit from the consumption of the money and while the repayment may work a hardship, it certainly cannot be considered as an "inequitable" one.

b. *Bona Fide Purchaser for Value*

The general rule today is that if an innocent purchaser takes property in good faith and without notice of any prior claims, his legal title will prevail over any other equitable interests. This was unlike the common law rule whereby a purchaser could not acquire good title to property without the consent of the owner. In order to prevail, the purchaser must acquire the property by purchase and pay value for it. But what if the situation involves two holders of equitable titles? For example, if an innocent purchaser bought land from a trustee who had not yet executed the deed. The innocent purchaser would have an equitable interest but so also would the beneficiary of the trust. Which of the two would prevail? If the equitable maxim "first in time, first in right" is applied, then the beneficiary would prevail. However, case law today supports the approach that equity will balance the hardships between the parties to determine which one will actually prevail.

Before any of the major rules can be applied, however, it must be established clearly that to be a bona fide purchaser, the purchase has to be made "without notice" of any prior claims. Under the Uniform Commercial Code, § 1–201, "a person has notice of a fact when he has actual notice or notification of it; or, he has received a notice or notification of it; or, from all the facts and circumstances known to him at the time in question he has reason to know that it exists." In § 3–304, "to be effective, notice must be received at such time and in such manner as to give a reasonable opportunity to act on it." Under what types of situations, therefore, can it be said that the purchaser either had notice or at least may be charged with it?

One such situation occurs under what is known as the doctrine of lis pendens, which stated briefly is that where the property in question is the subject-matter of an equity suit, the purchaser takes subject to the outcome of the suit, even though he had no actual notice and paid value. In the United States, the doctrine applies not only to all interests in land, but also, to chattels and other types of personal property except negotiable instruments.

Another situation closely allied to that of lis pendens concerns the recording statutes in the states which usually require that the commencement of a suit does not affect a bona fide purchaser for value unless a proper written notice of the suit has been filed in the appropriate registry of deeds or similar office. Similarly, the requirement to record equity decrees in the land records will have the same effect on subsequent purchasers as a recorded deed itself. In other words, such public records do constitute a form of constructive notice which will defeat the claim of the bona fide purchaser that he took "without notice." If the decree is not recorded, however, it will have the same effect as an unrecorded deed and will not be binding as notice to a subsequent purchaser.

Notice can also be garnered from the fact that a purchaser who knows that some one other than the vendor is in open and exclusive possession of the property, should at least force him to look into the possession. Where such is the situation the purchaser would be charged with notice of whatever he might have learned had he actually conducted a reasonable investigation.

In addition to the requirement of notice before one can be considered as a bona fide purchaser, there is also the requirement that the property must be obtained by giving value for it. If the vendee or grantee fails to give value for the conveyance, then he will take the property subject to any prior equities even though he had no notice of them. Further, with respect to value, is that requirement satisfied if the vendor deeds land to a creditor to satisfy a pre-existing debt or even mortgages it to him to secure that debt? Under the common law it was not considered to be a transfer for value; however, it is under § 3–112 of the Uniform Commercial Code which states that "The negotiability of an instrument is not affected by (a) the omission of a statement of any consideration . . . or (b) a statement that collateral has been given to secure obligations either on the instrument or otherwise of an obligor on the instrument or that in case of default on those obligations the holder may realize on or dispose of the collateral."

Finally, in order to be a bona fide purchaser for value, the vendee or grantee must obtain legal title to the property he seeks. He cannot be protected against unknown equities until he has actually become the true owner of the property. Using land as an example, there must be the payment of the purchase price and the execution of the deed. Once these have been accomplished subsequent notice of equities will be immaterial.

c. *Discharge for Value*

This defense is in the nature of an extension of the bona fide purchaser defense discussed above. In fact, upon examination, one could probably use the bona fide purchaser defense quite accurately for this same purpose. For example, assume that A mistakenly believes he owes money to B, who, upon tender of the amount by A, tells A to pay the money to C to satisfy a claim which C has against B. At this point, C receives the money from A without any notice of the mistake on the part of A in giving the money to C. He receives it for value because he gave up his claim against B in exchange for the money from C. The defense of being a bona fide purchaser for value seems to be fulfilled at this point; however, the release by C of his claim against B is called a "discharge for value" which C can use against any claim made by A to restore the money. It would appear, however, that before this defense can come into play, C would have to satisfy all of the requirements for being a bona fide purchaser for value.

d. *Volunteers and Intermeddlers*

Section 2 of the Law of Restitution (1937) brands the conduct of volunteers and intermeddlers as "officious" for which there is no recovery. As a general rule, whenever one person confers a benefit upon another intending it to be a gift he is considered to be a volunteer and is not entitled to restitution unless there was fraud, mistake, duress or undue influence. Further, with respect to mistake, the volunteer cannot claim restitution unless the other party either shared in or had knowledge of the mistake. Neither is protection given to a person who intermeddles in the affairs of another by paying another's debt without reason to or to obtain certain rights against the debtor without the consent of the creditor. An intermeddler cannot impose a benefit upon another which will enrich him and then seek to obtain restitution of the benefit for the simple reason that he did not give the defendant any choice in the matter. Recall the situation wherein the pool operator puts a swimming pool in the back yard of the defendant while he is absent. If he does this by bona fide mistake, he may be able to recover the value of his labor and materials or at least the amount by which the defendant's land is improved; however, if he does it to try to impose the sale upon the defendant who is not given any choice in the matter, he will fail for the reason that he is an officious intermeddler. There must be an opportunity given to reject the benefit and this is the general rule, although certain exceptions are made as in the case of a physician attending an accident victim. Here the law will impose a quasi-contractual relationship between the parties and allow the physician to recover the reasonable value of his services. Surely, under such circumstances, no one would consider the physician to be an intermeddler even if he failed to save the victim's life.

VI. RESCISSION

1. INTRODUCTION

As indicated in the previous chapter, rescission is either a legal or equitable action which normally involves restitution on both sides. It could have been covered in the previous chapter; however, because of its importance, it was felt that it deserved its own special treatment. At the outset, it must be understood that just as two parties have the right to contract without the aid of the courts, they also have the corresponding right to cancel or rescind their agreement without the aid of the courts. In other words, the first form of rescission is that by mutual agreement. Court delays would be prohibitive were that not the case. Once the parties agree to rescind, the next question that arises is what happens to the property or res which had been exchanged prior to the agreement to rescind? This is where the term "restitution" enters the picture. The purpose of rescission is to "undo" the contract, i.e., to restore the parties to their original positions. This can be done only if the parties restore the property or res they received from each other in implementation of the agreement which they later rescinded.

Moving now from rescission by mutual agreement to rescission which is desired by one party but refused by the other, just what can the plaintiff do to get the agreement rescinded and have his property restored to him? The first thing that the plaintiff has to do is to examine the facts of the situation at the time that the contract was made and see if there is anything which occurred at or prior to that time which could make the contract voidable. These items would be fraud, mistake, duress, illegality, impossibility of performance, or failure of consideration. For example, suppose A sells 100 crates of oranges to B thinking they are good when, in fact, they are rotten. This would be a mistake and as such it would be a ground for rescission—for "undoing the contract." If, on the other hand, in typing the contract, the secretary puts down "300" instead of "100" crates, this would call for reformation of the agreement, i.e., making the language of the agreement conform to the intentions of the parties. Reformation will be discussed in the next chapter; however, it is important at this time to understand that in reformation the purpose is to "keep" the contract rather than to "undo" it as in the case of rescission.

2. RESCISSION FOR MISTAKE

Equity will grant rescission for mutual mistake and unilateral mistake known to one of the parties but not for unilateral mistakes not known by the other party. What if only one party is mistaken and the other doesn't know of the mistake? If you rescinded on this basis, you could be defeating a "justifiable expectation interest" of the other party. The basic rule is that the right to rescission applies only to mutual mistakes of fact or to unilateral mistakes known to the other party, otherwise a "justifiable expectation interest" can be defeated.

Rescission will not be given to a unilateral mistake not known to the other party because this would defeat the "justifiable expectation interest" of the innocent party. There is one exception to this rule called the "Corbin" rule: If you find that the hardship to the unilaterally mistaken party is greater than the "justifiable expectation interest" of the innocent party, the contract should be rescinded even though the unilateral mistake is not known to the other party. Also, if in any unilateral mistake the parties can be put back to the pre-contract status quo, then rescission should be granted despite the profit or "justifiable expectation interest."

Rescission will not be granted, however, unless the mistake is a material one. It must go to the essence of the contract itself. Usually mistakes as to subject matter are material. If, on the other hand, the mistake goes to the value or quality, it would only be collateral and not material. A mistake as to the size of a lot is immaterial because it is not the essence of the contract. It is a collateral mistake going to quantity. But if the price is based on size, then it would be material. If the difference is small, the buyer can get a lower price; if it is too great, then he can get rescission.

In summary, therefore, the majority rule is that rescission will be granted for a mutual mistake of fact or a unilateral mistake of fact which is known or should have been known to the other party. There can be no rescission as long as there is a "justifiable expectation interest" to protect. A liberal minority rule states that rescission will be given for unilateral mistakes if the hardship out-weighs the "justifiable expectation interest." Finally, there is the modern rule which provides that rescission will be granted for any unilateral mistake so long as the parties can be restored to their pre-contract status quo.

3.   RESCISSION FOR MISREPRESENTATION

This is a good ground for rescission, but you must find it was a material misrepresentation and one of fact. It must be due to an express statement rather than to a non-disclosure. However, active conceal-ment is misrepresentation even though a party can-not ordinarily be said to *do* an act of concealment. Non-disclosure may also be misrepresentation if there is a duty to speak, e.g., fiduciary relationship or innocent misrepresentation which later turned bad so that the person has a duty to speak. You cannot have misrepresentation if it is merely an opinion unless a fiduciary relationship exists or the person making the opinion holds himself out to be an expert. In general, you should not rely upon the opinion of others, especially as to value; however, if the value statement goes to a fact, there can be reliance upon it. Misrepresentations of law are opinions and not facts and there should be no re-liance on these unless the person making them is an expert such as an attorney. The next question to ask is whether or not the misrepresentation is mate-rial. If it is fraudulent and the plaintiff relied upon it, it is material. If it is not fraudulent but innocent or negligent, you must find reasonable actual re-liance. "Reasonable" means that the person did some investigating himself and did not rely on certain misrepresentations. Or ask if a reasonable person would have relied upon it and then did the plaintiff so rely?

Is it necessary before rescission for fraud to prove that the other party should have known that the representation was false? The answer is in the negative because innocent misrepresentation can also be sufficient and is applicable in both law and equity. Actually, there is no distinction in the proof required either in law or equity with respect to the action for rescission; however, if the action is for damages as a result of the fraud, there must be proof of willful and fraudulent misrepresentation, made knowingly and resulting in damage. There will not be any recovery for the tort of fraud without showing injury to the plaintiff, even an award of nominal damages.

4. TYPES OF RESCISSION

Once the grounds for rescission have been established according to the above rules, there are two types of rescission available as remedies: Rescission at Law and Rescission in Equity. As indicated above, historically rescission was really accomplished outside of the court and the only thing left for the law court to do was to give the appropriate restitutionary relief. In equity, on the other hand, the rescission itself was actually accomplished by the decree.

a. *Rescission at Law*

Rescission at law begins when the plaintiff gives prompt notice of the rescission to the defendant and either restores to the defendant what he had received from him or at least makes a tender of it to the defendant. Once he does this, he is entitled to recover back what he gave the defendant and if the defendant refuses, the plaintiff can sue either in replevin for the chattels or in assumpsit if money is involved. It must be stressed that if the rescission is at law, the restoration of property belonging to the defendant by the plaintiff, or a tender of it, is a prerequisite to the action at law. The tender must be made unequivocally and in good faith. Once the plaintiff notifies the defendant of his intention to rescind and either restores the property or makes a tender of it and the defendant refuses to restore the plaintiff's property to him, the plaintiff posts a bond and the sheriff is ordered to seize the property from the defendant. At this point, the defendant must be notified of the impending seizure and must be given an informal hearing before the property is seized. If the hearing is in his favor, the defendant can then post a higher bond and hold the property until the formal hearing (Fuentes v. Shevin, 407 U.S. 67).

b. *Rescission in Equity*

The immediate difference between rescission at law and rescission in equity is that under the former theory the rescission is effected when the plaintiff notifies the defendant of his intention to rescind; whereas, in equity, the decision to rescind is the result of a judicial decree. In other words, in equity, the plaintiff agrees to restore any property or res belonging to the defendant and asks the court to order the defendant to return the plaintiff's property to him. Thus, the requirement of a prior or prerequisite tender is not necessary; however, students should be alert to the fact that most jurisdictions today require prompt notice and tender in both types of rescission.

When would a plaintiff seek rescission in equity rather than rescission at law? The usual case is where the rescission at law would be inadequate and this occurs when the equitable relief sought is the cancellation or execution of a deed to realty held by the defendant.

Are there any situations in which the tender is not necessary? The most obvious one is where what the plaintiff has is utterly worthless or if the plaintiff knows that the defendant would refuse it anyway; or if the plaintiff has consumed or used up that which he received from the defendant; or if the plaintiff has offsetting claims in money which are in excess of the money which the defendant is required to restore. If the item is no longer available, the plaintiff can tender its money value. If it is land, it must be restored with an adjustment for its use.

c. Defenses

The normal defenses are laches, unclean hands, and election of remedies. With respect to the latter defense, i.e., election of remedies, the problem arises when fraud is involved. If the plaintiff is seeking damages for fraud, he is affirming the contract. If he is seeking rescission of the contract because of fraud, he is "undoing" the contract. Thus the remedies are inconsistent. If the plaintiff starts out by trying to rescind the contract and the defendant does not accept the offer to rescind, the plaintiff can drop the action to rescind and sue for damages instead. Some jurisdictions allow him to plead both actions, and then elect one as the trial proceeds. If, however, the plaintiff starts out by first seeking damages, this is held to be such an affirmance of the contract that he cannot later bring a suit for rescission. Finally, estoppel may be a defense if the plaintiff after learning of the facts which would justify rescission, continues the contract.

There are also situations in which the Statute of Frauds is attempted to be used as a defense. For example, if the contract is within the Statute and is, in fact, in writing, is an oral agreement effective to rescind it? The answer is in the affirmative provided the oral agreement conforms to the requirements of a contract. The main reason is that the Statute of Frauds does not refer to contracts of rescission. However, care should be taken where the contract has been partly performed by the transfer of real property. An agreement to retransfer would have to be in writing. The Restatement, Second, Contracts, § 222 states, "Notwithstanding the Statute of Frauds, all unperformed duties under an enforceable contract may be discharged by an oral rescission. The Statute may, however, apply to a contract to rescind a transfer of property."

VII. REFORMATION

1. INTRODUCTION

As with rescission, the subject of reformation could have been covered in the chapter on restitution since it is a restitutionary remedy. However, like rescission, it deserves its own special consideration. That first thing, however, which must be grasped is that in rescission the original contract is voidable for some reason such as mistake, misrepresentation, fraud, duress, undue influence, illegality, impossibility of performance, or failure of consideration. In reformation, on the other hand, there is a valid contract between the parties but it does not conform to their original agreement and they are asking equity to change it for that reason. At the outset, therefore, if the original agreement is voidable, the remedy is rescission rather than reformation.

The theory upon which reformation is based is that the parties did reach an understanding but, in reducing it to writing, some provision was omitted generally through mutual mistake and equity is now being asked to insert that provision. Therefore, equity does not, and will not, make a new agreement for the parties and will not add a provision on which they did not agree. It will not be granted unless the plaintiff shows clearly and convincingly that the contract as written does not reflect the true agreement as the parties mutually intended it to be. It will not be granted just upon a probability that there was an error. There must, in fact, have been an error and not just a showing that the plaintiff or his attorney made a mistake. Unless there is fraud, the mistake must be proven as one made by both parties.

2. GROUNDS FOR REFORMATION

The major reason for reformation is that the writing is not in accord with the prior agreement due to mistake or fraud. Mutual mistake is a good ground for getting reformation as well as unilateral mistake known to the other party. As with rescission, reformation will be permitted only if the mistake is a mutual one and not where it is a mistake of law unless the mistake would result in great hardship. If the mistake, however, pertains to the existence of the subject matter, there can be nothing to reform and the proper remedy would be rescission rather than reformation. If there is either fraud or innocent misrepresentation, the contract is voidable and as such cannot be reformed. It can only be rescinded.

What then are the grounds for reformation? The most obvious would be where the parties believed the instrument reflected their agreement when in fact it did not, as indicated in the previous example where the secretary recorded "300" crates when the parties had agreed upon "100" crates. Thus, reformation can take care of what is known as "draftsmen's" errors, i.e., those caused by reducing the agreement to writing. A second ground would be where one of the parties knows or has reason to know that it does not conform to the agreement and the other party does not know. In such a situation, equity will reform the agreement to that which the parties actually agreed upon. A third ground would be even if it was a mistake of law made by a draftsman, reformation will be granted to cause it to conform to the agreement of the parties. Where mistake is the ground, it must have been made when the instrument was being drawn and not when it was made. This is because a presumption arises from the instrument itself that it does, in fact, set forth all of the provisions upon which the agreement was made. If, therefore, the mistake is denied, then the burden is on the party alleging the mistake to prove that the written instrument does not fully state the agreement which they intended.

3. DEFENSES

a. Statute of Frauds and Parol Evidence

As a general rule, the Statute of Frauds does not prevent reformation where the instrument is required to be in writing even if the mistake can be established only by parol evidence. In these cases, the parties make an oral agreement which cannot be enforced because it should have been in writing under the Statute of Frauds; however, once it is reduced to writing, it can be conformed to the true agreement even though that was oral and unenforceable. In this same connection, if the reformation would add to the instrument, there is a minority rule that denies reformation because the Statute of Frauds requires the transfer of an interest in land to be in writing. On the opposite side, the majority rule is that the Statute of Frauds is not involved where the reformation reduces the size of the conveyance. With respect to the parol evidence rule, it has to be recognized that reformation does impinge upon it because it takes oral statements which were made prior to the final agreement and incorporates them in a writing which is at variance with those oral statements. Parol evidence, however, is always admissible, not to vary the terms of a deed, but rather to show the alleged mutual mistake and the true intention of the parties.

b. Other Defenses

Some of the standard defenses which are used in equitable actions are available in a reformation action as well, for example, laches, once the plaintiff learns of the mistake and fails to take action within a reasonable time with the resulting prejudice to the defendant. Another would be a bona fide purchaser for value who has had no notice of any mistake in the instrument. A third would be the expiration of an applicable statute of limitations from the time of the mistake itself. A fourth would be ratification by the plaintiff after learning of the mistake which would estop him from seeking the reformation. Or, in a related category, an assumption by the plaintiff of the risk of the mistake which would also serve to estop him from seeking the action. Finally, changed position of the defendant in reliance on the instrument itself.

VIII. SPECIFIC PERFORMANCE

1. INTRODUCTION

As with Rescission and Reformation, the remedy of Specific Performance is directly related to breach of contract actions as opposed to using these remedies against tortfeasors. It should be rather obvious that one does not "rescind a tort, reform a tort, or ask to specifically perform a tort." The remedies of Injunction, Compensatory Damages and Restitution are specifically appropriate against tortfeasors. In general, Specific Performance is a remedy by which the equity court can order the defendant to do what he promised to do under an agreement. In other words, the plaintiff gets the performance he wants rather than damages because the money is inadequate. It is applied generally in two types of situations: land contracts and unique chattels. The reason for using it with respect to land is because land is "unique." No piece of land is like any other piece of land. Therefore, when the plaintiff and the defendant make a contract for the sale of land (realty) and the defendant later decides not to go through with the agreement, the plaintiff has the choice of either suing in equity for specific performance or at law for damages. With respect to chattels, equity will also determine whether or not the chattel is unique, such as a coin or stamp collection. If so, damages would be totally inadequate and the court of equity would grant specific performance. It would not do so for the ordinary chattel for the reason that the plaintiff could obtain money damages for the breach and obtain the same chattel in the open market.

The earliest leading case on the subject is Pusey v. Pusey (1684), 1 Vern. 273. That case involved the possession of a horn anciently given to the Pusey family by the Danish King Canute. The next reported case pertinent is Duke of Somerset v. Cookson (1735), 3 P.Wms. 389. It involved the possession of an old silver patera bearing a greek inscription and dedicated to Hercules, which had been dug up on the Duke's estate. In Fells v. Read (1796) a suit was brought to recover a tobacco box of a remarkable kind which had belonged to a club. In all of these cases, the actual value was extremely small at that time; however, the courts decided that recovery turned upon "pretium affectionis" (an imaginary value put upon a thing by the fancy of the owner and growing out of his attachment for the specific article). It has been said that mere sentiment or personal desire for a particular object affords no basis for an equitable action; however, when that sentiment or desire is based upon facts and circumstances which endow the chattel with a special value, to the extent of "pretium affectionis," there is and can be no measure of damages in money.

Before considering the elements involved in specific performance, there is one other advantage to this remedy. Since it is an order of the equity court, it is backed by the enforcement powers of that court if the defendant refuses to obey the order. For such refusal, he can be cited for criminal contempt and even jailed. He can also be cited for civil contempt for continuing to refuse to obey the order and can be jailed until he does decide to obey it. In such an instance, it is said that "he has the keys to his freedom in his pocket." In other words, he can let himself out once he decides to obey the order of the equity court. These enforcement powers are one of the major reasons why plaintiffs seek equity court jurisdiction. They do not exist at law. It is also for this very reason that equity is so discriminating in its acceptance of cases and why it holds to the original basis of equity jurisdiction viz., IS THE REMEDY AT LAW ADEQUATE?

The fundamental principles which guide a court of equity in decreeing the specific performance of contracts are essentially the same whether the contracts relate to real or to personal property. Because of the fact that damages for breach of a contract for the sale of personalty are in most cases easily ascertainable and recoverable at law, courts of equity in such cases withhold equitable relief. But no inherent difference between real estate and personal property controls the exercise of jurisdiction. Where there is no adequate remedy at law, specific performance of a contract touching the sale of personal property will be decreed with the same freedom as in the case of a contract for the sale of land.

It would be well at this point to give the position of the U.C.C. with respect to specific performance.

Section 2–716 provides that "(1) specific perform-ance may be decreed where the goods are unique or in other proper circumstances. (2) The decree for specific performance may include such terms and conditions as to payment of the price, damages, or other relief as the court may deem just. (3) The buyer has a right of replevin for goods identified to the contract if after a reasonable effort he is unable to effect cover for such goods or the circumstances reasonably indicate that such effort will be unavail-ing or if the goods have been shipped under reserva-tion and satisfaction of the security interest in them has been made and tendered." The language of the article indicates quite clearly that a more liberal approach for specific performance of contracts of sale is used. It is not limited only to items which are unique; rather, "in other proper circumstanc-es," undefined, except where, for example, the buy-er "is unable to effect cover."

2. REQUIREMENTS FOR SPECIFIC PERFORMANCE

a. *Is There a Valid Contract?*

Is it definite and certain enough for specific per-formance? This is extremely important because equity cannot be expected to enforce either an inval-id contract or one which is so vague as to its terms that equity cannot determine just what it must order each party to do. In addition, how can equity be expected to punish a defendant for not perform-ing a contract which is unclear as to exactly what the defendant is expected to do under the court order? The safest rule to follow is to require more definiteness and certainty for specific performance than for the ordinary contract. For example, if the contract is for $10,000 "terms of payment to be arranged," a law court can give damages to the victim because it can assume a legal rate of interest on deferred terms. But if the victim wants specific performance, it is not definite because equity cannot force payment plan terms on a seller unless the buyer agrees to pay all cash. Or, if the contract does not give the dates on which the defendant must perform, it is not definite and certain; however, in this respect, equity today is becoming much more liberal in supplying a reasonable time. In this same connection, equity will examine business usage and custom to determine whether or not missing terms can be supplied; however, this is not done where the terms are major or material to the agreement.

It is well settled that before a court will decree the specific performance of a contract, the written agreement or memorandum must contain the essential terms of a contract, expressed with such certainty and clarity that it may be understood without recourse to parol evidence to show the intentions of the parties. Restatement of the Law, Contracts, § 370 states "Specific enforcement will not be decreed unless the terms of the contract are so expressed that the court can render with reasonable certainty what is the duty of each party and the conditions under which the performance is due." The terms must be such that neither party can reasonably misunderstand them. It would be inequitable to carry a contract into effect where the court is left to ascertain the intention of the parties by mere guess or conjecture, because it might be guilty of erroneously decreeing what the parties never intended or contemplated.

b. *Is the Legal Remedy Adequate?*

In previous chapters it has been stressed that from its earliest history, equity decided to act only where the remedy at law was inadequate. This was done also to resolve conflicts with the law courts as to jurisdiction. And even today in those states in which both law and equity are integrated, equitable relief is still governed by this same criterion.

The question of adequacy of the legal remedy MUST be discussed in any specific performance question. Since it involves a contract which has been breached by the defendant, the only remedy which is available to the plaintiff at law is that of money damages. Therefore, the question should be asked immediately: Would money satisfy the plaintiff for his loss? To answer this, one must look to the subject-matter of the contract itself. If it is land, money is inadequate because, as indicated above, land is unique—no piece of land is like any other piece of land. In such case, no money can adequately get the buyer's expectation interest. He cannot get the same piece of land anywhere else.

Assume that the buyer, in anticipation of the seller fulfilling his part of the agreement to convey land, contracts to sell it to a third party and then the seller breaches? A minority rule says that since the buyer wasn't going to keep the land anyway, money damages are adequate. The majority rule, however, is that the money damages are not adequate because the buyer still faces a suit by the third party. If the seller sues the buyer, the answer would be the same because of the doctrine of mutuality of remedies (also known as "affirmative mutuality"), on the basis that since the buyer can get specific performance, so can the seller.

Assume now that the agreement contains a liquidated damages clause. How does that affect adequacy? The minority rule is that if it is there, the legal remedy is adequate simply because the parties said so. The majority rule is that you must ask whether or not the liquidated damage clause was put in the contract as a reasonable alternative clause. Was it "to buy the land OR pay a certain liquidated sum?" The key is: does he have a choice? Is it a true alternative? If it is a true alternative, then the legal remedy is adequate. If, on the other hand, it is a threat to insure performance, the legal remedy is not adequate. The language has to be examined carefully. In most instances of liquidated damages provisions, the parties are unable at the time of the making of the contract to estimate just what the damages might be in case of a breach; therefore, they settle upon an amount which would appear to be reasonable at that time. If when the breach actually occurs they find that the damages are grossly disproportionate to the amount estimated as liquidated damages, that portion of the agreement may be void and the court will favor consideration of the actual amount of damages. The real test, however, is that of the true alternative because if they agreed that the payment of damages would be just as acceptable as performance, no court of equity will grant specific performance and the legal remedy will be considered as adequate.

The law is now well settled that a liquidated damages provision alone will not, in and of itself, be construed as barring the remedy of specific performance. For there to be a complete bar to equitable relief, there must be something more such as explicit language in the contract that the liquidated damages provision was to be the "sole" remedy.

If the agreement involves the sale of a chattel rather than of land, the general measure of damages is the difference between the market price and the contract price. Thus, money damages would be adequate unless the chattel was a unique one. For example, if it is a stamp collection, no amount of money will enable a person to replace those stamps.

Money damages are also considered to be inadequate if the estimate is difficult to make, such as in output or requirements contracts, or if the chattel is scarce at the time even though it is not unique or one of a kind. Where you have a combination of unique and non-unique items in the same contract, equity will give specific performance of the entire contract.

If the contract is for the sale of stock which is listed, equity will not grant specific performance because money damages are usually adequate. However, if the stocks are unlisted or if the plaintiff is seeking control of the corporation, the courts may grant specific performance.

You cannot get specific performance for contracts to make a will while the testator is still alive. If the testator is dead and land is involved, the plaintiff can get a constructive trust on the land and ask for quasi-specific performance. If it is for money or a non-unique chattel, money damages are considered to be adequate.

Ordinarily, breaches of personal service contracts are compensated at law by money damages. Specific performance is generally denied not only because of the difficulty of enforcing such a decree but also because of equity's reluctance to "force" individuals upon each other particularly in a working relationship. There are situations, however, in which the services contracted for are unique. In such cases, the contract contains an affirmative covenant stating that the employee will work only for the employer or a negative covenant that the employee will not work for anyone else. Where this covenant is breached, the remedy is that of a prohibitory injunction ordering the employee not to work for anyone else. This is to be distinguished from covenants which take effect after the termination of an employee such as not to work within a specified geographical area for a particular period of time. Injunctions can be enforced in these cases provided the covenant is not unreasonable as to space and time. If they are unreasonable, the courts consider such covenants to be an illegal restraint of trade and unenforceable.

The question of granting specific performance in third party beneficiary contracts is also dependent upon the adequacy of the remedy at law. In the ordinary situation, if the promisor failed to confer the benefit which the promisee intended for the donee beneficiary, the most that the promisee could expect would be nominal damages. This remedy at law would not be considered as adequate because it could not possibly carry out the intention of the promisee to confer a specific benefit on the donee beneficiary. If the intended beneficiary is of the creditor type rather than the donee, and the promisor does not perform, the creditor beneficiary can always sue the promisee on the original debt and the promisee can, in turn, sue the promisor for his actual damages. Thus, the remedy at law would be adequate and this is the minority view in this type of situation; however, the majority view sees in this a multiplicity of suits which is always a ground for granting specific performance.

The fact that the defendant is insolvent is not a ground for equity jurisdiction. The remedy is what is looked at. If it exists and is adequate, the fact that it may be difficult to attain is not the consideration. Hence, alleged insolvency with its inability to collect damages is no reason for granting specific performance on the grounds that the remedy at law is inadequate. Attention should be paid, however, to local state statutes which may decree equitable jurisdiction in such a situation. In addition, the U.C.C. in § 2–702 provides that "where the seller discovers the buyer to be insolvent he may refuse delivery except for cash including payment for all goods theretofore delivered under the contract and stop delivery under this Article (§ 2–705). Where the seller discovers the buyer has received goods on credit while insolvent he may reclaim the goods upon demand made within ten days after the receipt, but if misrepresentation of solvency has been made to the particular seller in writing within three months before delivery the ten day limitation does not apply."

The above situations constitute the most important ones pertaining to the question of the adequacy or inadequacy of the legal remedy. They are not intended to be all-inclusive; rather, they are intended to emphasize the necessity of insuring that the question of adequacy of the legal remedy is always asked of any factual situation involving the possible use of the equitable remedy of specific performance. The case law graveyard for dismissed equitable actions is heaped with the bones of "the remedy at law is adequate."

c. Is the Decree Feasible to be Enforced by the Courts?

The question of feasibility with respect to the decree issued by a court of equity cannot be separated from the question of jurisdiction. As indicated earlier, equity jurisdiction is primarily in personam—it acts against the person. As long as the defendant is before the court, it can order him to convey or pay, whether the land is before it or not. Of course, the ideal situation is to have the land and both parties before the court. If then the defendant refuses to obey the decree, there is no problem with feasibility or the ability to supervise the decree. The equity court can punish the defendant through its criminal contempt procedures and convey title to the plaintiff through a commissioner's deed. With respect to the use of contempt powers, a question may arise if the vendor is suing to obtain the purchase price. Can equity incarcerate a defendant under its contempt procedures for his failure to pay that price? The answer is equally in the negative because of prohibitions against imprisonment for debt; however, equity is not without a feasible remedy. It can order specific performance by foreclosing the vendor's lien.

While the ideal situation as described above is that of in personam jurisdiction, it does not mean that the court of equity is powerless to act or that it would not be feasible to issue a decree where the vendor is out of the jurisdiction of the court but the land involved and the vendee are within it. In such a case, equity can use the in rem jurisdiction which it possesses by giving constructive service of process to the vendor. Such a situation would not create any major problems for the equity court with respect to its ability to supervise such a decree. There is a problem however, where the vendee rather than the vendor is not before the court. This arises because if you examine the decree for specific performance it is ordering the vendee (in personam jurisdiction) to pay the purchase price to the vendor. If it does not have that in personam jurisdiction over the vendee, how can it enforce the decree? This type of situation, therefore, does raise a question of feasibility with respect to supervising the decree and for this reason such decrees are not issued. If they are, they are either void or unenforceable for lack of jurisdiction.

The final situation with respect to land would be where the land is not before the court but the vendor and vendee are present. This would be akin to the ideal situation described above. So long as the court has the parties before it, it can order the decree of specific performance and supervise it through its contempt powers, both criminal and civil. The latter would be particularly effective by keeping the vendee imprisoned until he decided to obey the decree.

Equity, as a general rule, will not decree acts which it cannot supervise. Supervision is a particular problem in building or repair contracts because the court does not possess the technical know-how, means, or agencies to know exactly what the contractor is doing or if he is doing it well.

Despite the problem involved in supervising the execution of such contracts, however, there are certain exceptions. For example, if the plans for the building are clearly defined or if there has been sufficient part performance so that supervision of the remainder is not too difficult, equity may undertake its completion by specific performance. Supervising the finishing of constructing a building is different from trying to enforce a contract to repair a building. Here the court must first adjudge what repairs are to be made and the time within which they are to be done. In other words, the court must determine what, when, and how, and then enforce performance by attachment. Then arises the question of whether there has been substantial performance and if not, whether the defendant had any excuse therefor. Besides, the remedy at law in such cases affords full redress for such injuries. Thus, there is no general rule that courts of equity will never enforce a contract which requires some building to be done. Where it has been done the building was built upon the land of the person who agreed to do it; the consideration was the sale or conveyance of the land on which the building was to be erected and the plaintiff had already by such conveyance on his part executed the contract; in all of them the building was in some way essential to the use, or contributory to the value of the adjoining land belonging to the plaintiff. The tendency in modern times has been increasingly towards granting relief, where under the peculiar circumstances of the case, damages are not an adequate remedy.

As discussed above, with respect to the question of legal adequacy, equity generally refuses specific performance of personal service contracts, except with respect to reasonable negative covenants. The same rationale applies in the area of feasibility because of the prohibition against involuntary servitude imposed by the Thirteenth Amendment. If a negative covenant is contained in the contract, or if it may be implied from the language of the contract, and the service is unique, equity can order the employee not to work for anyone else. Prominent examples are those in the sports area where star players want to jump from one team to another.

The court will not order the star to play for his employer but it will order him not to play for any other team. The issuance of such a decree is ordinarily because the player's talents are so unique that not to issue the decree would cause the employer additional harm. Recall the landmark case of Lumley v. Gye (118 Eng.Rep. 749 (1853)) in which the defendant was under a contract to sing for the plaintiff. The contract did contain a negative covenant which the court enforced by ordering the defendant not to sing for anyone else. There was clearly additional harm here to the plaintiff who could not possibly find any other talent to either compare or compete with the defendant.

It should be noted further with respect to Lumley v. Gye that the defendant's covenants were both affirmative and negative and both were broken. Thus, the defendant was liable for full damages at law, despite the decision against her in equity. Both the Restatement of Contracts, § 384 and the U.C.C. § 2–716 support this. Under the Restatement (1932), "Specific performance and compensation in money are not alternative remedies, and both forms of relief may be given in the same proceeding; but compensation will not be awarded for an injury that an existing decree is intended to prevent, and specific performance will not be decreed by the prevention of an injury for which there is an existing award of compensation." The U.C.C. provides that "The decree for specific performance may include such terms and conditions as to payment of the price, damages or other relief as the court may deem just." In such cases, the defendant generally complains that he cannot earn a living under such a decree. It can be pointed out, however, that he still has his contract with the plaintiff who is ready, willing, and able to let the defendant work for him. If the plaintiff is not, the defendant may have a valid defense against the issuance of the decree; otherwise, there is no problem with the feasibility of the court to supervise such a decree.

d. *Is there Mutuality of Remedy?*

Historically, specific performance would not lie unless mutuality of remedy was available to both parties at the time the contract was executed. Courts of equity, acting merely on equitable principles, would not lend their aid where the remedy was not mutual. Want of mutuality was always deemed to be a sufficient ground for refusing specific performance of a contract. Today, this defense has been rejected in almost all jurisdictions in favor of the Restatement view of a conditional decree.

The Restatement of Contracts (Section 372(1)), states, "The fact that the remedy of specific performance is not available to one party is not a sufficient reason for refusing it to the other party." Today, it is not essential that the remedy of specific performance be mutual. The modern view is that the rule of mutuality of remedy is satisfied if the decree of specific performance operates effectively against both parties and gives to each the benefit of mutual obligation or performance. It is not necessary to serve the ends of equal justice that the parties shall have identical remedies. Rather, equity will order the defendant to perform but only on substantial performance by the plaintiff. For example, if the plaintiff is suing for specific performance of a land sale contract under which the defendant has refused to pay, the equity court will compel the defendant to pay only on the condition that the plaintiff also conveys the property. This would be in the nature of a conditional decree.

e. Are All the Conditions of the Contract Satisfied?

The plaintiff cannot sue the defendant if the plaintiff's conditions are still outstanding. For example, A agrees to give title to B and B agrees to pay A on July 15. B tenders the money on that date and A refuses to convey the deed. These are concurrent conditions. They must either be performed or excused. The vendor must be able to give a marketable title or he cannot require the vendee's performance. In addition, he should have that marketable title at least on closing day and the defendant cannot ordinarily object about the title before that time. If, however, the defendant knows that there is a defect in the title which cannot possibly be corrected by closing day, he is not required to wait until then before objecting. And certainly, if the vendor sells the property to another while the contract with the vendee is still executory, the vendor cannot claim that he has until closing day to present a marketable title.

In order for a party seeking specific performance against another to prevail, he must show as a condition precedent to his obtaining his remedy that he has done or offered to do, or is ready and willing to do, all such acts as are required of him in the execution of the contract according to its terms. He must show himself ready, willing, desirous, prompt and eager.

If time is of the essence in the contract either expressly or by implication, the contract should be examined to see if it is wholly executory. If so, specific performance will not be given because the plaintiff has not yet performed, i.e., one of his own conditions was that of time. If it is partly executed, as where the defendant has made 18 payments on time and is late on the 19th one, equity abhors forfeitures and will excuse the condition where the delay is slight and the other party has not been harmed. If time is not of the essence, specific performance will be allowed as long as the seller is not harmed and as long as payment by the buyer is made within a reasonable time.

The general rule is that time is not of the essence unless the contract expressly so provides. The modern view in both law and equity, particularly with respect to real estate transactions, is that time is not of the essence unless the parties have manifested such an intent. The same rule applies to both construction and manufacture of goods contracts. Where such a provision is made expressly it is considered to be one of direct stipulation as opposed to that of necessary implication. In cases of direct stipulation, the general rule is that the contract must be completed on the day specified or an action will lie for the breach of that contract. Where it is not so specified, but can be necessarily implied, this determination is made from the circumstances surrounding the case, as, for example, where the property sold is required for some immediate purpose, such as trade or manufacture; or where the property is of a determinable character, as an estate for life. Unless in cases of direct stipulation or of necessary implication, time is not considered in courts of equity to form such a portion of the contract as either party can treat to be an essential part of it. Courts of equity make a distinction in all cases between that which is matter of substance and that which is matter of form; and if it finds, that by insisting on form, the substance will be defeated, it holds it to be inequitable to allow a person to insist on such form and thereby defeat the substance. Time may in equity be made of the essence of the contract in three ways viz., by considerations arising either from the nature of the property, or the laches of the parties, or express agreement. It is well settled that the vendee may expressly stipulate that beyond a certain time he shall not be bound. When time is expressly made of the essence of the contract, specific performance will not be granted to the vendor or purchaser who is not ready to perform at the day appointed, when there is neither waiver nor forfeiture. The words "time shall be of the essence of the contract," are frequently used, but no particular form of stipulation is necessary. The equitable maxim of "equity regards substance rather than form" controls in such situations.

If the buyer assigns his rights and the assignee then sues the vendor, there will be no problem as long as the assignee is paying all cash. But if he says "I'll pay a certain amount of cash and here is the balance in a note," has he satisfied the conditions? The general rule is that he has not and equity will not grant specific performance because it would have the effect of forcing a different debtor upon the creditor. If, however, the promissory note is secured by a purchase money mortgage, this could be enforced because in such a case, the creditor is not looking to the credit of the vendee but rather to the land as his security. This is the normal type of mortgage whereby the mortgagor gives a certain amount of money in cash and then executes a mortgage on the property to the mortgagee to secure the balance of the purchase price.

If there is a material defect in the agreement, the vendor cannot get specific performance. For example, if the vendee wants 500 acres of land and the vendor has only 100 acres, equity will not grant specific performance because the defect is a material one. If, on the other hand, the vendor should have 499 acres, the question of materiality still arises and if the vendee won't get substantially what he bargained for, the answer would still be in the negative. But, if despite that shortage, the vendee wanted specific performance, he could get it by an abatement in the purchase price even if the defect was material because he could waive the defect. It should be noted that in such a case, the vendee could get the specific performance whereas in the situation above, the vendor could not get specific performance unless he could deliver substantially what he promised in the agreement and the difference would be so slight as to be inconsequential and immaterial. Otherwise, equity would be forcing an entirely different contract upon the vendee. One test, which equity uses in such situations is to look to the intended use of the property by the vendee. If even the absence of one acre would materially affect the intended use of the property, equity will not grant specific performance to the vendor with abatement in the purchase price.

The Restatement of Contracts (1932) in § 374, provides that "(1) Except as stated in Subsection (2), specific enforcement will be refused if a condition precedent to the duty to be enforced has not been and cannot be performed and is not excused, or if a condition subsequent terminating the duty has occurred. (2) Specific performance will not be refused by reason of provisions in the contract which make the duty of performance depend upon conditions, precedent or subsequent, of such a nature that refusal of a decree will effectuate an unjust penalty or forfeiture, and if substantial performance of the agreed exchange is assured as required by the rule in § 373." Section 373 provides that "Specific enforcement may properly be refused if a substantial part of the agreed exchange for the performance to be compelled is as yet unperformed and its commencement or future performance is not well secured to the satisfaction of the court." It is elementary that "he who seeks equity must do equity," or that a party to a contract or those standing on his right to entitle them to a specific performance of the provisions of the contract which are to be performed for his benefit, must affirmatively establish that he has faithfully kept and performed, or is ready to keep and perform all the provisions of the contract which he is required to perform, for the benefit of the other party.

f. What are the Defenses to Specific Performance?

Any one of the following or even a combination of several, may be available as a defense: Statute of Frauds, laches, unclean hands, hardship, mistake, and misrepresentation.

If A "orally" sells a house to B or if A "telephones" the offer to B, the Statute of Frauds would in all likelihood arise. But suppose the statement is that A and B "enter into a contract." Just what does this mean? Is it oral or written? One should recall from his first section of Contracts that whenever an interest in land is involved, the agreement should be in writing. The student should also recall that part performance of an oral contract pertaining to land will create an exception to the Statute of Frauds on either the evidentiary or the estoppel theory. Under the evidentiary theory, the acts performed relate so closely to the contract that one can conclude that there is in fact a contract. Under the estoppel theory, the vendee, acting on statements or conduct by the vendor, undertakes certain acts which will constitute a hardship on his part unless the vendor is estopped from asserting that the agreement is not in writing. Usually, in this respect, there are three elements which should be considered: possession, payment, and improvements. The standard rule with respect to payment is that it is not sufficient to take the contract out of the Statute of Frauds because the vendor can return the money and the parties are placed in the position of status quo. The majority rule with respect to possession alone is that it is not sufficient to take the agreement out of the Statute of Frauds, although the Restatement is contrary to this majority rule. The making of improvements alone would also not be sufficient to take the agreement out of the Statute of Frauds since the vendor could pay the vendee either the reasonable or actual value of such improvements. The solution, then, is a combination of these factors. The most ideal situation would be payment, possession, and making improvements. However, case law supports a combination of any two of these factors. Thus, improvement plus possession would be sufficient; or payment plus possession.

The Restatement, Second, Contracts (1968), Section 197 states "A contract for the transfer of an interest in land may be specifically enforced notwithstanding failure to comply with the Statute of Frauds, if it is established that the party seeking enforcement, in reasonable reliance on the contract and on the continuing assent of the party against whom enforcement is sought, has so changed his position, that injustice can be avoided only by specific enforcement." It should be noted that there are

[135]

four states in which no acts of part performance will be recognized to take an oral land contract out of the Statute of Frauds. These are Kentucky, Mississippi, North Carolina and Tennessee.

If the land sale contract involves that section of the Statute of Frauds dealing with contracts which cannot be performed within one year, careful attention should be paid as to whether or not the Statute of Frauds can be satisfied through compliance with the interest in land section of the Statute. For example, if the contract provides that the deed is not to be delivered until well after the one year limitation in the Statute, will payment and possession or possession and making improvements take it out of the Statute? The general rule is that if two sections of the Statute are involved, compliance with one section will also satisfy the other. In other words, if possession and making improvements would take the agreement out of the Statute, then the fact that the "beyond one year" section is also involved will not prevent the oral agreement from being enforced. As in any other instance, an examination should be made of pertinent state statutes. Some statutes provide that the "one year" section is not applicable to land contracts since such is governed by the "interest in land" section of the Statute.

As mentioned earlier, "equity aids the vigilant, not those who slumber on their rights." This is known as the equitable defense of "laches" which is not peculiar to specific performance but is applicable to all forms of equitable actions. It is invoked where a party has delayed his action *unreasonably* and that delay has caused *prejudicial* harm to the defendant. In this respect it differs from the Statute of Limitations which is concerned primarily with the passage of a fixed period of time beyond which an action cannot be brought. In laches, there is no fixed period of time, although a good rule of thumb to follow is that the Statute of Limitations is the outside maximum for laches. Since "equity regards substance rather than form," it does not tie itself to a specific period of time, particularly the mere passage of that time. Rather, it looks from the time that the plaintiff has actual knowledge that a right has been infringed. In this respect, if the plaintiff delays unreasonably, equity may well hold that his action is barred even though the comparable Statute of Limitations has not yet run. Secondly, the delay must be prejudicial to the defendant before he can invoke laches as an equitable defense. The question, therefore, is not just what is the amount of time involved, but rather, what is the effect of the passage of time? Case law also supports the proposition that where the time period of the Statute of Limitations has been met or exceeded, the burden of proving prejudice which is originally upon the defendant, shifts to the plaintiff to show why laches should not be invoked. A showing of prejudice or change of position is necessary if the period of delay relied upon by the defendant is less than the limitation period applicable to the legal remedy which is available for the defendant.

"He who comes into equity must come with clean hands." This maxim of equity represents what is called the "clean hands doctrine." As a defense, it is available in all equitable actions, not just specific performance. It has one major limitation which must be understood clearly in order that the doctrine may be applied correctly. The uncleanness must arise out of the *same transaction* upon which the plaintiff is suing. The "same transaction" is actually the problem in applying the doctrine. The defendant cannot bring in any other criminal or tortious conduct on the part of the plaintiff unless it arises under the "same transaction" which is the issue in the suit, neither does it have to be fraud. It can be something amounting to fraud as long as it is founded in the same transaction; however, if it is fraud, then the defendant should use fraud as his defense.

Under Contracts law it should be recalled that the question of adequacy of consideration is not a major problem in determining the existence of a contract. The majority rule in the United States is that any amount of consideration, no matter how slight, is sufficient as long as the other elements of legal detriment or benefit are present. It should also be recalled, however, that the courts do look to the adequacy of consideration where the question of hardship is involved. The general rule in such situations is that if the inadequacy is so gross as to shock the conscience, then it will be hardship. In other words if the inadequacy is coupled with an unconscionable contract, it would be hardship. Equity, then, in such cases, looks to see if one side, usually in a superior bargaining position, is trying to take unfair advantage of the other party. This situation occurs where the inadequate consideration is coupled with "sharp dealings" or "sharp practices", as where the plaintiff is urged to sign when he is infirm or sick. It must .be remembered however, that neither law nor equity will make a new contract for the parties. While it may be sympathetic to a party who has made a bad bargain, that fact alone does not constitute hardship. Further, in determining whether or not hardship does exist, the majority rule is to look at the factors, particularly the adequacy of the consideration, as they existed at the time of the making of the contract and not later.

Inadequacy of price may, of itself, and without fraud be sufficient to stay the power of a court of equity to enforce a specific performance of a contract to sell land; however, mere inadequacy of price, independent of other circumstances, is not sufficient to set aside the transaction. If the inadequacy is so great as to give the character of hardship, unreasonableness, and inequality to the contract, specific performance can be refused and the plaintiff left to seek his compensation in damages. Equity will not refuse to decree specific performance solely on the grounds of inadequacy of consideration. Finally, one should be alert to the fact that hardship, unclean hands, laches, and the Statute of Frauds can easily overlap in a given situation.

Mistakes and misrepresentations which are a basis for rescission as discussed in Chapter VI, may also be a basis for defense against specific performance. It should stand to reason that if the mistakes or misrepresentations are sufficiently material to rescind the contract, they should also serve to prevent its specific performance. Where the misrepresentations have caused the defendant to believe that he does not have to perform under the contract, and he so relies, equity will estop the plaintiff from denying the misrepresentations.

Section 2–217 of the U.C.C. provides that "(1) Specific performance may be decreed where the goods are unique or in other proper circumstances. (2) The decree for specific performance may include such terms and conditions as to payment of the price, damages, or other relief as the court may deem just."

The application of the above criteria to a contractual situation should provide the pattern necessary for determining whether or not specific performance is the proper remedy to be sought. Its specific application, particularly in the area of Equitable Conversion, is discussed in Chapter XIV of this book. The above represents a schematic or checklist for both the student and the practitioner with respect to the remedy of specific performance.

SECTION "B"

THE REMEDIES—HOW THEY ARE USED

IX. REMEDIES FOR INJURIES TO REALTY, PERSONAL PROPERTY AND MONEY

1. INTRODUCTION

The purpose of this chapter and those which follow in this section is to apply the rules of remedies discussed in the previous section. It is designed only with the purpose of accomplishing the desired object of student utility. Now that the basic rules of remedies have been given, their usefulness would remain abstract without a practical discussion of their application. As a general rule, all remedies have one basic goal and that is to put the plaintiff in the position he would have been in had the contract been performed or the injury not occurred. It is not to make him rich and even where punitive damages are awarded, the object is to punish the defendant and try to deter him—it is not to enrich the plaintiff. As each item or situation is discussed, the applicable remedy or remedies will be presented.

The term "tangible interests," has been applied generally by some writers to three categories of property—land, personal property, and money. These would be contrasted with "intangible interests" dealing primarily with business interests such as infringement of patents, copyrights, trademarks, commercial disparagement and unfair competition. Whether the damage to the tangible interest is in tort or contract, it is necessary to first determine the extent of the owner's interest, and insure that this is compensated for whatever damage has been done to it. The older cases tried to establish a single measure of recovery for whatever damage was done but the courts today recognize that the recovery should be related to that part of the owner's interest which has been injured. For example, if it is a nuisance, it violates the owner's right to the quiet enjoyment of his property. Compensation for this in the form of damages may be totally inadequate and only an injunction may serve to protect that interest. A trespass on the other hand, could also interfere with the quiet enjoyment of the property particularly if it is a continuing one. If not, the damage caused by the ordinary trespass would probably be to the value of the property itself, particularly if it went beyond the mere crossing of another's property otherwise nominal damages would be sufficient to protect the right involved. In just about any such case, the one in possession can usually recover nominal damages.

Where the injury goes beyond that of nominal damages, the court usually applies one of two basic measures of damages when dealing with injuries to tangible interests. The first is that of diminished value which is the value of the item immediately before and immediately after the injury. The second is that of replacement value, which is the cost of restoring or repairing the item involved. The problem arises when there is a question of which measure to use. If the damage to the property is of a permanent nature, the courts are inclined to use the diminished value test for the rather obvious reason that replacement costs would probably not restore the plaintiff to the position he was in prior to the injury to his land. There is also the consideration that the costs of replacement or repair may far exceed the value of the property and end up putting the plaintiff in a much better position than he was in before the injury occurred. For example, if the damage is to an old barn building which prior to the injury by a bulldozer had a limited or minimal value and the costs of restoring the damaged walls would have the effect of actually enhancing the value of the building, the courts generally refuse to apply the replacement cost measure. Here again, one must resort to the basic goal of damages which is to put the plaintiff in the position he was in prior to the injury. It is not to enrich him at the expense of the defendant. To resolve this problem, some courts state that the replacement or repair costs cannot exceed the diminished value. This has the effect, however, of putting a ceiling on the recovery and is analogous to the contract price or a liquidated damages provision in a contract which can serve as a ceiling for recovery where there is a breach of the contract.

2. INJURIES TO LAND

Case law over the years has developed certain specific rules of remedies which one can expect to be applied in certain types of cases. At least sufficient precedent has been established for either the student or the practitioner to get a "handle" on the applicable law involved and then adjust or modify it to the specific factual situation. These situations are discussed in the following subparagraphs.

a. *Trespass*

The standard rule is that every unauthorized entry upon land is a trespass. It will be direct if the entry itself is direct such as walking onto the land, throwing something directly onto it, shooting over it, or digging under it. It will be indirect if something is being done on another's property which spills over to a neighbor's property. All that is necessary to bring the action is to be in possession of the property. If it is a simple trespass, such as walking across the land of another, where no physical injury to the property results, the plaintiff can recover nominal damages to protect his right to the enjoyment of his property. If while walking over the land, the defendant kicked over a flower bed, the injury would be a temporary one, and the measure of damages would be the replacement costs of the flower bed. If on the other hand, the injury was a permanent one such as the destruction of valuable trees, the remedy would then be the diminished value of the land. Now let's assume that the defendant is walking over the plaintiff's property every day. This would constitute a repeated or continuing invasion of the plaintiff's property and each time that he did this, the plaintiff would have a new cause of action and the Statute of Limitations would run anew with each invasion. Where such is the case, the plaintiff can apply the same rules as to simple trespass, i.e., if the injury is temporary, sue for all replacement costs up to the time of the trial. If, on the other hand, it looks like it is going to continue indefinitely, then consider the diminished value in the land as a measure. Where the trespass would be considered as "permanent" rather than repeated or continuing, there is only one cause of action and the Statute of Limitations begins to run from the time the invasion began. Under this, the plaintiff should sue for all damages up to the time of trial, including prospective damages, based upon the diminished value of the land.

In addition to the damages mentioned above, claims for trespass can be increased either through special or punitive damages or damages provided by state statutes. If the trespass causes emotional harm, particularly the intentional infliction of mental distress, recovery may be had for that injury also. If the trespass caused the plaintiff to lose the use of his property, then a fair rental value of the land could be imposed. Finally, if the trespass was either wilful or malicious, punitive damages may be recovered. A question which usually arises in this respect is whether or not punitive damages may be recovered in addition to multiple damages provided by statute. Case law does not provide a clear-cut answer to this situation because some courts consider the multiple damages to be severe enough whereas other jurisdictions feel it is necessary to impose both to deter the defendant.

One of the grounds for seeking injunctive relief is that of multiplicity of suits. If the trespass is purely a simple one, the courts will consider the remedy at law to be adequate and will deny injunctive relief. If, however, the trespass is a continuing one which will result in a multiplicity of suits, as where the defendant leaves something on his neighbor's property or fails to remove it when he should, the remedy of diminished value may not be adequate and equity would issue an injunction to enjoin future trespasses and to prevent the multiplicity of suits. There is one caveat which should be mentioned concerning such injunctions, particularly those of a permanent nature affecting trespass. Generally, equity will not issue injunctions where the title is in dispute. In fact, equity tries to avoid trying title to land unless the inadequacy of the remedy at law would justify it. One way of avoiding this is for equity to issue a preliminary injunction until such time as the title dispute is settled at law. Another method which seems to indicate a modern trend is for equity to impanel a jury in the same lawsuit and resolve the question of title. This method is applicable particularly in situations where the defendant is in possession of land belonging to the plaintiff who is seeking an injunction to oust him from such possession. Normally, equity does not transfer possession of real estate by any type of injunction, preliminary or permanent. The remedy for this is specific performance. Care should be taken, however, to distinguish this from the situation in which the defendant attempts, in bad faith, to take possession of a portion of the plaintiff's property either by force or by means of an encroaching structure. In such cases, equity may order the defendant to remove the encroaching structure, thereby returning possession of the plaintiff's property.

b. *Encroachments*

An encroachment is a continuing trespass which occurs when the defendant builds a structure which is partly on his land and partly on that of the plaintiff or builds it all on his land with the exception of an overhang which extends over the land of the plaintiff. If the defendant erected the structure intentionally knowing that it impinged on the land of the plaintiff, equity will grant an injunction ordering him to tear it down. In all other situations involving good faith, where the encroachment, for example, has been made by mistake, the court will balance the hardships between the parties. Economic waste is a predominant factor in this consideration. Once the court determines that the encroachment was done in good faith, equity hesitates to allow the defendant to buy that portion of the plaintiff's property covered by the encroachment. Rather, a more equitable solution is to limit the action to granting an easement to the defendant so that the plaintiff can later recover that portion of his land when the encroachment is removed.

c. *Ejectment*

Up to this point, the emphasis has been on either the casual trespasser or one who makes repeated and continuous invasions of the property of another. What if instead of just walking across the plaintiff's property, the defendant actually takes possession of it and occupies it? If the situation occurred at the common law and the plaintiff wanted the defendant put off the land, he brought an action at law in ejectment. Before a judgment could be given, however, the question of title had to be resolved in that action. In addition, the plaintiff brought a second action for what was called "mesne profits." Today, there is no necessity to bring both actions since that for "mesne profits" is now included in the action for ejectment, and includes such items as a rental value for the property while it was in the hands of the defendant, plus any profits or rents that he might have received during the occupancy less his own expenses so that the plaintiff receives a "net" type of award. If the trespasser entered upon the land in good faith and made certain improvements on it, he would not be required to pay for the added value of his own improvements, and there is case law supporting the idea of giving the increased value of the land to the innocent trespasser or allowing him to remove the improvement.

d. *Forcible Entry and Detainer*

The term "forcible entry and detainer" actually contains two types of action—one for "forcible entry" to oust an occupant of land and the other of "unlawful detainer" or holdover by one who is in possession of land. It has been said that there is no "private domain" authority given to individuals. Society could not exist with any degree of cohesion if citizens possessed the right to move indiscriminately onto the land of others, particularly with the use of force, and oust the occupants. On the other hand, once land is occupied even under a valid lease and the occupants refuse to leave at the expiration of the lease, this would constitute "unlawful detainer" of the property on their part. There are remedies at law to cover both situations, and provide both damages and recovery of the property.

Most states have a summary process of eviction statute to cover the situation involving unlawful detainer. While the process is becoming more complicated through the use of multiple forms, it usually takes only three days to obtain the writ and have it executed by the sheriff. One of the added advantages to using this particular remedy is that, unlike ejectment, title is not in issue.

Under the forcible entry statutes, there is a minority rule which states that the occupant and his property can be expelled provided only reasonable force is used. The majority rule holds that a forcible entry on land, even by the owner, will be invalid as a privilege and the occupant can recover for assault and battery if any force is used. There is one major exception: if a trespasser ousts the owner, the trespasser will acquire no such possession as will entitle him to protection if the owner re-enters immediately, even though the entry may involve the use of force.

It would appear that the legal remedies for forcible entry and detainer are adequate so that equity can continue its traditional reluctance to issue injunctive relief where such is the case or where title may be involved.

e. *Nuisance*

Nuisance is in effect a form of trespass to land because it is in the private sense an unreasonable interference with one's use and enjoyment of his land. Trespass and private nuisance, however, are separate fields of tort liability relating to actionable interference with the possession of land. They may be distinguished by comparing the interest invaded. An actionable invasion of a possessor's interest in the exclusive possession of land is a trespass; an actionable invasion of a possessor's interest in the use and enjoyment of his land is a nuisance. The same conduct on the part of a defendant may and often does result in the actionable invasion of both of these interests, in which case the choice between the two remedies is, in most cases, a matter of little consequence. Where the action is brought on the theory of nuisance alone, the court ordinarily is not called upon to determine whether the conduct would also result in a trespassory invasion. In such cases the court's treatment of the invasion solely in terms of the law of nuisance does not mean that the same product could not also be regarded as a trespass.

A public nuisance is an interference with the interests of the community or of the general public. It can relate to the use of public lands such as highways, or public health such as the failure of health officials to keep ponds from being polluted, or public safety, such as the failure to enforce leash laws on vicious animals, or even such items as public comfort, morals and convenience. Ordinarily, a private citizen cannot sue for a public nuisance unless he shows injuries and damages greater than those for the ordinary citizen.

In general, nuisances can be either intentional, negligent, or even a form of strict liability. Some jurisdictions divide nuisances into those "per se" and those "per accidens." In these jurisdictions, those designated "per se" are considered to be absolute, i.e., without regard to the care with which it is exercised or the conditions under which it exists. For example, in those jurisdictions, a funeral home would be considered a nuisance "per se" whether located in a residential or commercial area. The better view is to avoid such "absoluteness" and determine the type of nuisance from the surrounding circumstances. Such is a nuisance "per accidens", which occurs by reason of circumstances and may be found where the natural tendency of the act is to create danger or inflict injury on person or property. Another distinction between a nuisance "per se" and one "per accidens" is that in the former, injury in some form is certain to be inflicted, while in the latter, the injury is uncertain or contingent until it actually occurs. If, however, the injury which is anticipated is imminent and certain to occur, it may be enjoinable as an anticipatory nuisance.

In order for the injury to constitute a nuisance, there must be substantial interference with the enjoyment and use of the land; actual possession or the right to it; and the harm should be over an extended period of time. Contributory negligence, assumption of risk, and abatement of the nuisance are good defenses to such an action.

Every person is bound to make a reasonable use of his property so as to occasion no unnecessary damage or annoyance to his neighbor. If he makes an unreasonable, unwarrantable or unlawful use of it, so as to produce material annoyance, inconvenience, discomfort or hurt to his neighbor, he will be guilty of a nuisance to his neighbor and the law will hold him responsible for the consequent damage. As to what is a reasonable use of one's own property, this cannot be defined by any certain general rules, but must depend upon the circumstances of each case. A use of property in one locality and under some circumstances may be lawful and reasonable, which, under other circumstances, would be unlawful, unreasonable, and a nuisance. To constitute a nuisance, the use must be such as to produce a tangible and appreciable injury to neighboring property, or such as to render its enjoyment specially uncomfortable or inconvenient.

Whenever a nuisance may be involved, the first thing to consider and examine is the physical invasion itself. Is it something which is likely to continue more or less indefinitely? For example, will the pollution of the stream by the chemical company never end? Will the plant which is spewing tarred smoke against the neighbor's property continue indefinitely? If so, the nuisance is probably a permanent one, the measure of damages for which is the depreciation in the value of the land. If the nuisance can be abated, the measure is the depreciation in the rental or use value during the time that the nuisance exists plus special damages. If the nuisance causes actual injury to the property, recovery can be for the replacement value or repair costs. The plaintiff can also recover the cost of abating the nuisance and can generally get special damages for his own discomfort and illness. Another remedy is to see if the court will issue a limited injunction permitting the defendant to experiment to see if the abatement will correct the situation.

In just about every situation involving nuisance, the court takes economic waste into consideration and balances the hardships between the parties. Would it work a greater hardship on the defendant to issue the injunction and thus cause him to close down his plant than to deny the injunction to the plaintiff, thereby giving the tortfeasor an easement to continue to commit the nuisance?

The ground for denial of an injunction in nuisance cases can be the large disparity in economic consequences of the nuisance and the injunction. Where this occurs, one alternative is to grant the injunction but postpone its effect to a specified future date to give opportunity for technical advances to permit the defendant to eliminate the nuisance; another is to grant the injunction conditioned on the payment of permanent damages to the plaintiff which would compensate him for the total economic loss to his property present and future caused by the defendant's operation. As with other forms of trespass, awards can also be given for punitive damages particularly where the wrongdoer is acting in bad faith and maliciously.

In some situations, the defendant will try to avail himself of a specific zoning ordinance which would have the effect of authorizing the nuisance. Zoning regulations are issued today because of the complexity of the society under which we live. They are necessary to an orderly concept of living as are traffic regulations; however, there is nothing absolute or fixed about zoning regulations. They must be examined according to the circumstances of the situation to which they apply. Generally, the legislatures take these into consideration when developing such regulations. For example, a restriction as to the height of a building may be extremely valid in an urban area, whereas, it would be inapplicable and invalid in a rural community. Similarly, a zoning regulation along our highways and freeways to either eliminate or minimize the use of billboards in order to emphasize the esthetic value of the countryside would also be a valid exercise of that power.

Based upon such considerations and their applicability to local circumstances, what is the rule with respect to issuing injunctions where the defendant claims his protection under a zoning regulation? The majority rule is that such regulations will not prevent the issuance of an injunction against a nuisance because it has been determined that zoning ordinances are worded fairly general in nature. Thus, it does become a matter of interpretation and there is no automatic license given to the defendant to perpetrate a nuisance under its aegis. There is a minority view to the contrary, but even in those jurisdictions which follow it, damages have been awarded to the plaintiff for the nuisance.

f. Waste

There are two types of waste—voluntary and permissive. Voluntary is active waste committed by a tenant, while permissive is his failure to keep the property in a state of good repair. In other words, he lets it "run down." The damages for waste, particularly of the voluntary type, are generally controlled by state statutes which award as high as treble damages. Consideration, however, should be given to the extent of the damage to the property to see if the replacement or repair cost would be a more appropriate measure of recovery. Where the plaintiff becomes aware that the tenant is actively committing waste, he may seek a prohibitory injunction to prevent greater damage from occurring. This is contrasted with permissive waste in which the courts do not ordinarily grant injunctions on the grounds that much of the damage constitutes wear and tear on the property aggravated by the tenant's failure to take the immediate steps to keep it in good condition. There is also the question as to whether or not the tenant will actually restore the condition of the property before he vacates the premises. The ordinary measure of damages, therefore, for permissive waste is either replacement costs or diminished value of the property.

The student should be aware of two caveats with respect to waste. The first is that it can be committed only by one who is rightfully in possession of land. Therefore, a trespasser cannot commit waste. Second, waste in addition to constituting some type of destruction to the property can also be in the form of causing improvement to the property in which case it is called "ameliorative waste." For example, suppose the landowner has an old barn building on his property which is extremely unsightly and totally unfit for economic repair. As it stands, it has a depreciating effect on the value of the land. The tenant in possession causes the barn to be destroyed and removed so that he actually improves the value of the land. Some jurisdictions hold that in such cases, there is actually no waste at all. Others, and these are in the majority, hold that it is still waste and the tenant should be held for at least the increased taxes resulting from the improvement in the value of the property.

g. Severance

The question of the particular remedy for the severance of materials from land, such as minerals, timber, crops, sand, dirt, or gravel, depends to a great extent on the manner in which it is done, i.e., the good or bad faith of the trespasser. This is true particularly where such damages are provided by statutes which usually designate treble damages for bad faith cutting and double damages for good faith cutting. In such cases, the burden of proof that it was done in good faith is on the defendant. If, on the other hand, the plaintiff is seeking punitive damages, the burden is on him to show that the defendant acted in bad faith. These rules, of course, raise the question of just what constitutes "good faith?" One approach is to put it on the basis of knowledge, i.e., the trespasser knows when he is acting in good or bad faith. But what if he is acting under the mistaken belief that he has title to the property? What if he failed to check the records to determine just who did have title? In either of these cases, particularly the one concerning mere negligence, the courts have held that these are not sufficient to put the trespasser in the category of bad faith. On the other hand, his failure to make a required survey has been the basis for a bad faith imposition of damages.

What is the effect on a subsequent purchaser of one who has trespassed in bad faith? The general rule is that he also is liable for conversion and pays the value of the item at the time that he purchased it from the bad faith trespasser. If, on the other hand, the trespasser did so in good faith, the subsequent purchaser pays only the same as the trespasser, e.g., in the case of severance of timber, this would be the stumpage value. With these general rules in mind, the specific remedies for severance as indicated, are as follows.

(1) Minerals

If the severance is done in bad faith, the general measure of damages is the value of the mineral removed without any deduction for the expenses in extracting it. If it is in good faith, it is the value of the mineral in the ground, i.e., its value at the mouth of the mine less the costs of extraction. Some courts allow only a royalty which is the amount a miner would pay the owner to mine at so much per ton; however, most courts follow the value-less-cost-of-extraction rule.

(2) Timber

If the severance is in bad faith, the wilful trespasser pays enhanced damages. If it is in good faith, then it is the stumpage value. Reference should be made to state statutes in this respect, particularly in those states which have a high timber industry and are protective of those interests. Such states generally provide for treble damages where the cutting is done in bad faith and double damages where it is done in good faith.

(3) Crops

If the crops are destroyed, the measure of damages is the value at the time and place of destruction. If they are only injured, it is the diminished value at the time and place of injury. One of the major problems here is that growing crops have no market value. In such cases, the courts award the market value of the lost portion as measured at the maturity of the crop less the cost of harvesting and marketing the lost portion. Other jurisdictions use the rental value of the land with the cost of reseeding.

(4) Fruit Trees

In this situation, the victim can use either the separate value of the destroyed trees or the diminished value of the land as the measure of damages.

(5) Sand and Gravel

If these are removed in good faith, it is the value of the sand or gravel in place. If it is removed in bad faith, it is the value when screened.

(6) Dirt

The measure of damages for the removal of dirt from one's property is either the diminished value of the property as a result of the removal or the replacement cost of the dirt.

(7) Buildings

If the building is destroyed, the measure of damages would be the value of the building at the time of destruction. This could be determined by taking its original cost less depreciation or its replacement cost less depreciation. If, on the other hand, the building is damaged, then the measure of damages would be the replacement costs unless it was economically wasteful to repair. One way of avoiding this problem is to limit the recovery to the diminished value of the property. Consideration should also be given to the loss of use of the building while it is being repaired.

3. INJURIES TO PERSONAL PROPERTY

a. General

Unlike the previous section which involved the use of land and, therefore, in most cases, provided equitable relief, the subject of personal property has remedies at law which are adequate unless the chattel itself is unique. Particularly in this respect equity will ask the question: Is the remedy at law adequate? Where, for example, the owner of an ordinary piece of personal property has it wrongfully taken or withheld he can bring either detinue or replevin to recover the property itself. Under replevin, the plaintiff files his action to recover the property and posts a bond guaranteeing that the defendant will be reimbursed for damages if the court finally decides that the property does belong to the defendant. When the sheriff receives the bond, he notifies the defendant who, today, is given an informal hearing before the property is seized, at which hearing, the defendant can post a counter-bond which guarantees that he will pay the plaintiff certain damages should the plaintiff win. With such a guarantee, the defendant can have the property re-delivered to him until the final determination as to title is made. Ordinarily, this procedure at law is adequate unless the property is unique or the inherent delays in the procedure cause undue injury to the plaintiff. For example, when the plaintiff posts his bond, the sheriff does seize the property from the defendant; however, he must hold it either until the trial or until the defendant has an opportunity to post the counter-bond and have the property re-delivered to him. Also, the sheriff may not be able to go out immediately to seize the property, or the defendant may have it at a different place or he may deliberately hide it or even destroy it. In any of these situations, the remedy would be inadequate and the plaintiff may well seek equitable replevin under which a preliminary mandatory injunction would be issued to the defendant ordering him to deliver the property to the plaintiff and backing up the order with the contempt power of the court itself. The trial, thereafter, would decide the final title to the property, although equity would have made a preliminary determination of that fact when it issued the preliminary mandatory injunction.

Where the defendant does detain the chattel and exercises domination over it to the prejudice of the plaintiff, the tort involved is that of conversion, the damages for which would be the value of the item as of the time and place of conversion. If no market place is available, then the one closest to it, less any costs of transportation could be used to determine that value. If, on the other hand, the detention does not amount to a lengthy appropriation of or dominance over the chattel, the action should be treated as mere trespass to chattel, the damages for which would be the loss of use or even nominal damages where there is no actual injury to the plaintiff. One such situation for awarding nominal or only special damages would be where the plaintiff recovers his chattel "in good shape." The return by the defendant would mitigate the damages he owes to the plaintiff; however, there is a caveat that the owner cannot be compelled to take the chattel back and so the mere tender is not in and of itself a mitigating circumstance, except, perhaps, in the case of punitive damages because it does show good faith on the part of the defendant.

b. Special Damages

The plaintiff is also entitled to special damages in conversion actions. The most obvious one is that of loss of use of the chattel during the time that it was detained by the defendant. The question which arises here is: what measure of damages is to be used for loss of use? This, in turn, finds a problem in the fact that in the ordinary conversion action, the defendant pays for the value of the property which is in effect a forced sale upon him by the plaintiff. When that occurs, hasn't the plaintiff been reimbursed sufficiently? Some courts hold exactly that way unless the plaintiff had rented a replacement during the period of the detention, in which case, the defendant would pay the rental costs of the replacement in addition to the value of the detained chattel. In replevin, however, the plaintiff is seeking the return of his property in specie and also damages for the detention. One of those damages would be where the goods have a usable value. In other words, where the plaintiff can show that he intended to use the goods, for example, in his business. Where he can do this, the plaintiff would ordinarily recover a rental value as the measure of damages for such goods during the period of detention by the defendant. Can interest also be recovered as a special item of damages? Interest is appropriate based upon the value of the goods. Can he recover for emotional distress connected with the conversion? Generally yes, if the conversion is associated with malice or bad faith. It is traditional for courts to avoid payment for intentional infliction of mental distress unless connected with another tort. What about expenses for trying to recover the converted property? These are proper as special damages and are usually covered by state statutes. Under these, even rewards paid to encourage others to recover the property are reimbursable.

c. *Punitive Damages*

Punitive damages are awarded in conversion cases particularly where the taking was malicious and in bad faith. Actually, unless the defendant can show a mistaken belief or some form of good faith, there is almost a presumption that the wrongful taking or wrongful detention of the chattel was malicious and in bad faith. As in all other situations, punitive damages are within the discretion of the court.

d. *Waiver of the Tort*

As indicated earlier, the plaintiff should examine the facts carefully to see if he wants to elect to waive the tort and sue instead in assumpsit. This type of action is extremely important from a remedies standpoint because it reaches the unjust gains of the defendant, particularly where he has sold the chattel. If, for example, the action is in the tort of conversion, the measure of damages is the value of the item at the time and place of the conversion.

On the other hand, suing in assumpsit will give the plaintiff the proceeds of the sale. In using this action, however, attention must be paid to the common law counts which accompanied assumpsit. If the defendant has in fact sold the goods, the common law count of "money had and received" would be the appropriate one. If he had not yet sold the goods, the common law count of "goods sold (to defendant) and delivered (to him)" must be used. Here again, if the goods are sold, the measure of recovery would be the proceeds of the sale. If not, it would be the value of the goods at the time and place of conversion.

e. *Equitable Actions*

There are two major equitable remedies which may be used in the case of conversion. These are the constructive trust and the equitable lien. If the facts indicate that a fiduciary relationship exists between the parties, there would be no problem whatsoever in holding the defendant as a constructive trustee of the proceeds for the plaintiff. If this relationship does not exist and the conversion was not accomplished through fraud or duress, the legal remedy of replevin will probably be adequate particularly where the defendant has not disposed of the goods by sale. Where they have been sold, equitable replevin may be the better action to reach the unjust gains resulting from the sale. In any event, and providing that there is compliance with the requirements therefor, particularly that of tracing, an equitable lien might be imposed to protect the interests of the plaintiff over unsecured creditors.

f. Specific Applications

Using the above general rules pertaining to personal property, the following specific applications will be examined so that the student will have a frame of reference within which he can maneuver.

(1) Personal Property Destroyed

Where the chattel is either destroyed or damaged beyond repair, the general measure of damages would be the market value at the time and place, or nearest, of the destruction, less the cost of transporting the chattel to the nearest market. What is meant by the "market value?" This has variations depending upon the person who has been injured. For the average buyer or consumer, the market value would be the item's retail value so that he could go back into the market to replace the item if he so desired. If the plaintiff is a retailer himself, then the market value would be the wholesale price which would enable him to sell the item again at the retail price. If it is the manufacturer, he gets his selling price. This means that he gets his profits whereas the retailer does not. In addition, the plaintiff may also get the loss of use during a reasonable time for a replacement. The measure for the loss of use is the cost of renting a substitute on the market; or the value of the use of the chattel itself as if it had not been damaged. If there is no appropriate market value, then the actual value to the owner or the cost of repair may be used with an appropriate deduction for depreciation. These arise particularly in the case of vehicles which are damaged beyond repair in accidents. Some courts refuse to give loss of use damages where the chattel is destroyed but the trend today is to make the award particularly where the plaintiff moves quickly to obtain the replacement vehicle in order to minimize damages.

(2) Personal Property Damaged

The basic measure where the property is damaged rather than destroyed, is the depreciation, i.e., the difference between the value before and the value after the damage. Another measure would be the cost of restoring the property to its pre-damaged condition. But does this actually occur? If an automobile is in a serious accident, can the repairs put the car in the same condition as it was before the accident? It is doubtful even from a mechanical standpoint. Further, once a future buyer knows that the vehicle was involved in the accident, he is most reluctant to purchase it despite the assurances given concerning the repairs. This is perhaps the best argument for using the depreciation measure of damages. The plaintiff can also get loss of use damages while the vehicle or chattel is being repaired. This is usually measured by the cost of a substitute replacement or if a substitute cannot be obtained, then the loss of profits as a result thereof. The plaintiff must be aware in such a situation of the avoidable consequences rule under which he is required to minimize the damages due from the defendant. For example, if he fails to get a replacement vehicle on the basis that his lost profits will soar and he will be able to obtain these from the defendant, the courts will refuse to allow any recovery beyond what is considered to be a reasonable time in which the plaintiff should have obtained a replacement.

(3) Clothing or Household Furnishings

The general rule here is that the measure of damages is the value to the owner rather than the market value. The difficulty here lies in a determination of just what is the "value to the owner?" Obviously, it cannot be determined without an opinion from the owner as to its actual or real value to him. Further, there does not seem to be any real reason why the market value of the clothing or household furnishings would not be adequate. In either event, the householder would replace the item from the existing market and would want at least that value for the damaged or destroyed chattel. It would seem that the better measure would be the market value of the chattel less depreciation. After all, if the washing machine is five years old at the time of destruction, there is no valid reason for giving the plaintiff the full market value to purchase a brand new one just because he testifies that such is the "value to him."

(4) Stocks

Stocks represent a particular problem because of the fluctuation of the market. If they are converted, the basic measure of damages for conversion can be applied, i.e, the market value at the time and place, or nearest, of the conversion. But what if the plaintiff is not aware that his stocks have been converted until a time when the market has risen and he expects to make a "killing" only to discover that the stocks have been misappropriated fraudulently or even stolen? Is the market value at the time of conversion a fair measure of damages for him particularly when the wrongdoer may have sold the stock at a much higher price? To offset these situations, the courts have fashioned several other measures of damages. One of these would be the highest value between the date of the conversion and the date of the trial. This rule would at least give the plaintiff the advantage of any favorable fluctuation of the market during that particular time. Another, which is known as the New York Rule and is more widely used today than any of the others, is the highest value between the date the plaintiff had notice of the conversion and a reasonable time thereafter for replacement. This corrects the initial problem of the plaintiff not knowing that his stock has been converted and then gives him a reasonable time thereafter to select a market condition in which he would have sought a favorable replacement rate.

(5) Money

Money, from the standpoint of being a chattel or personal property, when misappropriated, may be the subject of a conversion action although some courts prefer to waive the tort and have the plaintiff sue in assumpsit for money had and received. If the misappropriation is done by a fiduciary, the plaintiff can resort to the equitable remedies of constructive trust or equitable lien rather than assumpsit which is the action at law. The value of using the equitable remedies lies in the fact that the money can be traced into another product and either the constructive trust or equitable lien imposed upon it. For example, suppose that the fiduciary embezzles the funds and then purchases stock or a home with them. The plaintiff can trace his funds into either the stock or the home and place a constructive trust on either for his own benefit. Thus the wrongdoer becomes a trustee, holding the property for the benefit of the plaintiff. This then has the effect of preventing the embezzler from profiting by unjust enrichment. If the fiduciary embezzles the money and then uses it to make improvements on his own property, the constructive trust would be inappropriate but the equitable lien could be used. The additional value of the constructive trust lies in the fact that it would give the plaintiff a priority over any other creditors of the fiduciary, whereas if the action were brought in conversion or assumpsit, the plaintiff would have to share with all the other creditors.

The major difficulty which arises with respect to money is the tracing requirement when using either the constructive trust or the equitable lien. Specifically, how can the money be traced once it is commingled with that of the wrongdoer? Or what if the wrongdoer uses all of the plaintiff's money and then deposits his own in the same account? Has he restored the fund? If this is his intent, the new deposit would be treated as the plaintiff's money and would be called the "lowest intermediate balance" which would not be subject to the claims of all other creditors. Over the years, the courts have attempted various solutions to the problem of tracing the plaintiff's funds in a commingled account. These approaches have been summarized earlier in section 5 of Chapter IV on Restitution.

X. REMEDIES FOR INJURIES TO PERSONAL INTERESTS

1. GENERAL

The previous chapter in describing the application of various remedies to what has been characterized as "tangible" interests, appeared to relate the remedy to the item itself. For example, if land was involved, the remedy was directed either to the diminished value of the land or its replacement cost to put the land in the condition it would have been in had the injury not occurred. The same direction appeared to be followed with respect to personal property, including money. In other words, injury to the object itself rather than to the person who owned the object, provided the rationale for determining the appropriate remedy.

The items to be covered in this chapter, while themselves "tangible" in the sense that they possess physical characteristics, seem to derive their remedy not from themselves as objects, but rather because of the benefits which they confer upon a person. For example, where a patent on a particular invention is involved, the objects, i.e., the patent and the invention, are both "tangible" interests; however, the law protecting them is designed to allow the inventor to receive a reasonable expectancy of reward for his ideas which have been translated into something "tangible." Whenever, therefore, there has been an infringement of that patent by a wrongdoer, there is also a diversion of the benefits which the victim expected to receive. It is to the protection of this personal right and expectancy that the remedy must be directed rather than to the object itself. This observation is made in full recognition of the fact that the application and use of the word "tangible" probably is in accord with the requirement of equity to find a property interest which it can protect when issuing its decrees. The recognition of the personal right involved, however, is more in accord with the modern trend to eliminate the fictionalization of the property right. With this understanding in mind, this chapter will concern itself with appropriate remedies for interference with contract, infringement of trademarks, trade names, patents, copyrights, various forms of unfair competition torts, personal injury and death, defamation and related wrongs.

2. INTERFERENCE WITH CONTRACTUAL AND OTHER RELATIONSHIPS

In the leading case of Lumley v. Guy, the plaintiff had a contract with a talented singer to perform for him. The defendant induced the singer to breach that contract and sing instead for him. The court stated that his inducement of the breach constituted a tort. This is the normal situation involving interference with a contractual relationship. It involves first a contract of employment usually with a negative covenant. Second, the contract involves a person, one of exceptional talent or skill whose services are usually sought by a competitor, who is even willing to resort to bribery to convince the "star" to perform for him. When this occurs and the employee does breach the contract, the employer has two causes of action—one in contract and the other in tort and he generally can plead both. As far as the contract action is concerned, the employer would be entitled to the market-contract price differential when he obtained the services of another employee. In addition, he would be entitled to any costs expended in training the new employee. The tortfeasor who induced the breach would be held liable for these same general damages. The question of special damages on the contract action would depend upon the rule of foreseeability announced in the landmark case of Hadley v. Baxendale which limited recovery to those which were contemplated by the parties at the time the contract was made. It is for this reason that the plaintiff may elect the action in tort rather than in contract. He can still recover the general damages he would have in the contract action but he would not be limited to the foreseeable damages in the tort action because liability in tort is imposed for all consequences resulting from the tort whether they were foreseen or not. There is a minority view which would limit the tortfeasor's liability for special damages in the tort action to those which were foreseeable. This has the effect of applying the contract limitation of foreseeability to the tort action. Damages for mental suffering and punitive damages are also recoverable in the tort action against the tortfeasor whereas they are generally denied in the contract action.

One way of solving the problem is to sue both parties in the same suit as joint tortfeasors. Both then would be subject to the judgment and the plaintiff could have his choice of collecting from either one of them. If the action is brought in contract, the majority rule is that punitive damages cannot be recovered; however, there are a limited number of jurisdictions which hold that a separate suit can be brought for the punitive damages and res judicata is not a defense because the issue of punitive damages was never before the court in the contract action.

A specific problem may arise where the contract contains a liquidated damage clause as the "sole remedy" for any breach. Where this is the case, does the amount in the contract operate as a ceiling even for the tortfeasor and despite the fact that he was not a party to the contract? There is very little case law on the subject but what there is answers the question in the affirmative.

The equitable actions of constructive trust and equitable lien may be invoked particularly where the tortfeasor induces a fiduciary to breach his contract or trust as where he convinces him to disclose trade secrets. If, as a result, the tortfeasor realizes a profit from his wrongdoing, a constructive trust would be imposed on it for the benefit of the plaintiff. There is even authority that it would be imposed in the absence of a fiduciary relationship provided that the tracing requirement was met. Finally, the equitable remedy of injunction is available to the plaintiff particularly where a negative covenant is involved. The injunction would not order the employee to work for the plaintiff but it would order him not to work for anyone else.

[174]

While the employment contract situation is the one usually considered when the subject of interference is involved, the student should be aware that the court is beginning to extend it to other situations not involving employment contracts. For example, assume that Company A and Company B are competing for an award of a sewer cleaning contract with City X; that Company A receives the contract; that Company B is a bad loser and dumps additional garbage and refuse into the sewers so that Company A will not realize any profit on its contract with City X. If Company A explains this to City X and refuses to go ahead with the contract, City X can sue Company A for anticipatory repudiation of the contract. In such a case, the courts have permitted Company A to sue Company B in tort for intentional interference with a contractual relationship. The damages would be those which would enable Company A to carry out its contract with City X while still receiving its expectancy under the contract. In fact, equity could issue a mandatory injunction to Company B to remove the refuse it deposited deliberately in the sewers or pay Company A the costs of having it removed.

In either of the situations described above, the remedies are directed toward protecting the benefits which the plaintiff expects to receive under his contractual relations and which have been diverted because of the intentional action of the tortfeasor. It should be noted that such expectancies arise from the existence of a contract. Can the plaintiff recover for an interference with an expectancy in the absence of a contractual relationship? For example, if the plaintiff is a businessman who expects to make sales to potential customers, can he recover from another who commits a wrong which will cause the customers not to deal with the businessman? The majority rule is that if another so interferes with trade, he may be treated as a tortfeasor if he does so intentionally. The general category for such interference is called "unfair competition" which is discussed in § 4 of this chapter.

An area that is specifically prone to having anticipated benefits diverted occurs when one who knows that he is to take under a will commits a wrong against the testator to prevent him from changing his will so that the wrongdoer would in fact be disinherited. This occurs when the potential heir uses fraud or undue influence on the testator or even murders him. Where this occurs, the majority of the courts denies the murderer any benefits under the will and imposes a constructive trust on the inheritance to hold for the benefit of other members of the family. It should be noted that there is no contractual relationship between the testator and the wrongdoer. Rather, the wrongdoer by his act of preventing the testator from changing the will, diverted expected benefits from the new heir. The use of the constructive trust has a restitutionary effect which prevents the wrongdoer from profiting by his unjust enrichment. Most courts apply the same type of ruling to situations involving co-tenants, one of whom murders the other. Some States following the Restatement of Restitution, § 188 (1937), impose the constructive trust on the entire amount of the property but allow the murderer to retain one-half of the income for life. Others allow the murderer a life estate in the entire property, while still others impose the constructive trust on only half the property, thereby allowing the murderer to keep the remaining one-half. Finally, some states hold that the killing converts the co-tenancy to one in common and the murderer is entitled to keep only as much of the property as he put into it. The student is advised to consult his state statutes in this matter because of the diversity of rulings in most jurisdictions.

Another area in which interference with a contractual relationship can cause problems is that of marriage and the family. The weight of authority is against the issuance of an injunction against interference with the relationship between husband and wife. The main reason is that equity normally does not function without finding some property right to protect. In family relationships, it is the personal rights of the parties which are involved. This does not mean, however, that the courts will not act in all such instances. For example, the family relationships can be severely interfered with where personal injury is caused by an outsider, particularly where the victim has been the main provider of support to the family. The rules affecting this type of action are discussed in § 4 of this chapter and the related causes of action are brought under such statutes. Another example would be that involving an unemancipated minor who is obligated to turn his earnings over to the family. If an outsider should induce the minor to leave home, thereby depriving the family of those earnings, he may well find himself paying damages for the interference.

Another area of contractual relationship into which equity hesitates to intrude is that of associational membership. Originally, equity's hesitancy to examine the admission practices of associations confined itself to social clubs, religious organizations and fraternal organizations. Today, equity is more inclined to intervene in the affairs of a private association if the admission practices affect the excluded person's ability to earn a livelihood. Equity does not hesitate to intervene, however, where a member who has been admitted, is now expelled apparently without being given due process. This is particularly true where the expelled member's property rights to certain benefits, such as death benefits or his right to employment may be lost by the dismissal. These would give equity the property rights they desire and once the plaintiff had exhausted his administrative remedies with the organization equity would determine if the dismissal proceedings conformed to the rules of due process.

3. REMEDIES FOR UNFAIR COMPETITION AND RELATED TORTS

Unfair competition, as its own tort, was developed to protect the goodwill of a business. As such, remedies were given for the "palming" or "passing" off of products by one competitor as though they were the products of another competitor who happened to be the true owner and originator of those products. This "palming off" would not only confuse the buying public but tend as well to be misleading. The tort was later expanded to include "misappropriation" cases particularly where the defendant obtained a "free ride" on the efforts of the plaintiff in developing his products. The leading case in point involved a news service on the west coast which copied news items printed by a competitor on the east coast. This time differential enabled the west coast printer to "ride free" on the work of the west coast publisher whose reporters all over the world gathered the items and sent them into their office on the east coast. Not all jurisdictions follow the "misappropriation" theory primarily on the grounds that a property interest in the material is lacking. Related torts which will be discussed in this section, include patent infringements, copyright violations, trademark and trade name infringements, right to publicity, commercial disparagement, trade secrets, and commercial bribery.

a. Patent Infringements

In 1964, the Supreme Court decided in the case of Sears Roebuck Co. v. Stiffel Co. (376 U.S. 225) that neither a federal nor a state court can prohibit the copying of an article which is on the market nor award damages for such copying if the article is unpatented or uncopyrighted. In other words, without a patent or copyright, a manufacturer cannot prevent a competitor from copying his product right down to the last detail. There are at least 3,800,000 patents which already have been issued in the United States and about 80,000 are issued each year.

Each patent has a lifespan of seventeen years and where an infringement occurs, searches are limited to the seventeen years preceding the search.

An individual should file for a patent if his product is new and has commercial value. His application is filed with the U.S. Patent Office where it is thoroughly reviewed by an Examiner. After a search, the application may be rejected by the Examiner who cites prior patents and publications in his decision. If the application is accepted, it is effective for seventeen years from its date of issue. Since patents are issued in the United States to individuals, not to companies, most companies enter into a written agreement with their employees in which the employees grant all patent rights for their inventions to the company. Novel ornamental objects can be protected with respect to their appearance by what are known as "design patents," for from three and a half to fourteen years.

The question of appropriate remedies for patent infringement must begin with the fact that exclusive jurisdiction over such cases is vested in the federal courts (35 U.S.C.A. § 266 et seq.). In general, the statute provides for injunctive relief, damages (up to treble the amount), attorney's fees in exceptional cases and interest. Consideration for issuing an injunction has the same basis as that for issuing any injunction, i.e., a showing of irreparable harm to the plaintiff. In addition, there must be a showing that the patent is valid and this has to depend to a great extent on the patentability search which must be undertaken to insure that there are no patents which anticipate the invention no matter how old the patents may be. In many cases, someone else may have a pending patent application for a similar product. The Patent Office does not grant access to pending patent applications, many of which are pending for several years. As a result, there is the possibility that a patent covering the product might be issued to another person some time after the search was completed. Where this occurs, evidence has to be introduced to show that the person claiming the patent infringement was in fact the first inventor of the product. If the validity of the patent is not upheld there can be severe damage to the defendant whose reputation may have already been ruined as a result of any preliminary injunction which may have been issued.

Damages "adequate to compensate for the infringement" are authorized by the statute, which sets as a minimum award a sum no less than "a reasonable royalty for the use made of the invention by the infringer." It also authorizes the damages to be increased up to three times. The problem which arises with respect to damages is whether or not all of the profits made by the defendant can be recovered by the plaintiff. The answer is in the affirmative where the entire marketable value of the item is dependent on the patent; however, where the patented item is tied in with a non-patented item, the question of monopoly may arise where the patentee is using his patent right to force a licensee to accept or purchase non-patented items. Where the statute uses the royalty fee as a minimum form of compensation, it refers to the fee which a patentee would charge a licensee to use the patent. This, of course, would have to be based upon expert opinion as to the expected profits of the licensee. Some courts, on the other hand, consider the actual profits of the infringer as a basis for determining the royalty fee. The amount of the royalty and the date of its effectiveness as a fee are important in determining the interest which is specifically authorized by the statute. As a general rule, the interest will run from the time that the royalty should have been paid.

Under the pre-1946 patent statutes, the patentee was allowed to recover the infringer's profits by way of restitution to prevent his unjust enrichment. The infringer was deemed to be holding the profits in a constructive trust for the patentee. The statute today eliminates all reference to the recovery of profits and seems to limit the recovery to injunction and damages. It would appear that the plaintiff today can reach the profits of the defendant by showing these as losses to himself rather than as gains by the defendant. This can be done by showing that customers who purchased from the infringer would have purchased from the patentee had the infringement not occurred.

b. *Copyright Violations*

A copyright is created by publishing an original work with the proper copyright notice and then having it recorded in the Copyright Office in the Library of Congress. The copyright itself protects the form or language that is used in the document rather than the ideas as such. A competitor may use the substance of the thoughts presented in creating his own publication. He cannot use the exact form or specific language of the original publication. Copyright protection lasts for the life of author plus 50 years. Like the patent, copyrights are within the exclusive jurisdiction of the federal courts per statute in 17 U.S.C.A. §§ 1–215 and 28 U.S.C.A. § 1338. In general, remedies for violations include damages, injunction, restitution, attorney's fees, interest and punitive damage.

While the basis for issuing injunctions follows that for all other injunctions, they are relatively easier to come by than in the case of patent infringements. In fact, once the plaintiff makes out a prima facie case of infringement he is ordinarily entitled to a preliminary injunction. At the final hearing, once the likelihood of future infringement is established, a permanent injunction will be issued. In addition, the statute authorizes the impoundment of all articles which infringe the copyright plus any items which were used to produce the articles. All of these may be confiscated and destroyed.

The subject of damages under the copyright statute is far more complicated than under the patent statute, because it authorizes several types of damages. The first type are those which the plaintiff would ordinarily suffer from the copyright violations, i.e., those which flow naturally from such infringement. Next are those "in lieu of" actual damages in sums not less than $250 nor more than $10,000 where the violation was innocent. If the infringement is wilful, the ceiling could be that of $50,000 but in such a case the character of the defendant's conduct must be taken into consideration. Finally, there is a "compulsory licensing" provision whereby anyone who records the music of a composer must pay the owner two and three-fourths cents per recording or one-half cent per minute of playing time whichever is greater (17 U.S.C.A. § 115).

The determination of the ordinary damages for copyright infringement can be made by considering the copyright as property and giving the plaintiff the difference between the value of the copyright before infringement and its value after infringement. Or, the actual loss by the plaintiff rather than the diminished value may be used. Special damages, while not stated specifically in the statute, may be recovered if they are proven with certainty and are not too remote from the violation. It is important to note that with respect to the "in lieu of" damages, i.e., not less than $250 nor more than $10,000, these can be awarded particularly where no damages have been proven although there is case law to support the discretion of the trial judge in awarding "in lieu of" damages instead of other ordinary damages. Finally, the statute contains a schedule of royalties which provides guidance to the court but is not binding upon it.

Unlike the patent statute, the copyright statute does provide for the recovery of the infringer's profits. In other words, this statute does provide for restitution based upon the gains of the defendant and to prevent his unjust enrichment. Thus, the infringer may be liable both for losses suffered by the plaintiff and gains made by the infringer because of the violations or infringement. When the statute speaks of "profits" it refers to "net profits" although in the ordinary case, all the plaintiff has to show is the gross profits and the defendant must prove that he is entitled to certain expenses which can be allocated or apportioned to his own efforts, overhead, and income taxes but only if the wrongdoing was not in bad faith. In any event, the burden is on the infringer to show that certain portions of the profits should be allocated to his non-infringing activities. Any doubts in this respect will be resolved against him.

The copyright statute provides specifically that full court costs will be allowed and that attorney's fees "may" be allowed. Punitive damages are authorized where the infringement is malicious and while interest is not specifically mentioned in the statute, post-judgment interest from the date of judgment may be given.

c. *Trademark and Trade Name Infringements*

Unlike the laws of patents and copyrights, those of trademarks and trade names are not exclusively federal. The common law did protect trademarks which were used by manufacturers to identify the source of their goods.

The redress that is accorded in trademark cases is based upon the party's right to be protected in the good will of a trade or business. The primary and proper function of a trademark is to identify the origin or ownership of the article to which it is affixed. Where a party has been in the habit of labeling his goods with a distinctive mark, so that purchasers recognize goods thus marked as being of his production, others are barred from applying the same mark to goods of the same description, because to do so would in effect represent their goods to be of his production and would tend to deprive him of the profit he might make through the sale of the goods which the purchaser intended to buy. Courts afford redress or relief upon the ground that a party has a valuable interest in the good will of his trade or business, and in the trademarks adopted to maintain and extend it. The essence of the wrong consists in the sale of the goods of one manufacturer or vendor for those of another. The essential element is the same in trademark cases as in cases of unfair competition unaccompanied with trademark infringement. In fact, the common law of trademarks is but a part of the broader law of unfair competition. Common law trademarks and the right to their exclusive use, are, of course, to be classed among property rights but only in the sense that a man's right to the continued enjoyment of his trade reputation and the good will that flows from it, free from unwarranted interference by others, is a property right for the protection of which a trademark is an instrumentality. In short, the trademark is treated as merely a protection for the good will and not the subject of property except in connection with an existing business. In the ordinary case of parties competing

[186]

under the same mark in the same market, it is correct to say that prior appropriation settles the question. But where two parties independently are employing the same mark upon goods of the same class but in separate markets wholly remote the one from the other, the question of prior appropriation is legally insignificant, unless it appears at least that the second adopter has selected the mark with some design inimical to the interests of the first user, such as to take the benefit of his goods, to forestall the extension of his trade or the like. The general doctrine is that equity will not only enjoin the appropriation and use of a trademark or trade name where it is completely identical with the name of the competitor, but will enjoin such appropriation and use where the resemblance is so close as to be likely to produce confusion as to such identity to the injury of the competitor to which the name belongs.

The common law also protected trade names which came to be associated in the minds of the public with particular manufacturers in quality and reliability. When this occurred, such trade names acquired a "secondary meaning"; therefore, unlike trademarks which became effective when affixed to the product involved, trade names did not become effective until they acquired this "secondary meaning".

At the federal level, the Lanham Act (15 U.S.C.A. § 1051 et seq.), provides for the registration of both trademarks and trade names. Such registration is considered to be constructive notice to all others of the owner's claim and the fact that he is the first user of either the trademark or trade name. It must be emphasized, however, that federal registration of the trademark is not necessary before it becomes effective for purposes of suit for infringement. Trade names, however, cannot be registered until they acquire their "secondary meaning". The first step which should be taken to register either the trademark or the trade name is to make sure that a similar mark has not been registered or applied for in the United States Patent Office. Once this has been determined, the manufacturer can apply for registration which is usually completed within one year. Once this registration has been granted, it is renewable at twenty year intervals. If no one contests the mark within five years after registration, the manufacturer can file an affidavit to have the right made incontestable. A trademark may be registered for a service as well as a product and once it has been registered the manufacturer can then use the phrase "Registered U.S. Patent Office" on all labeling and advertising. This marking entitles the manufacturer to collect damages from an infringer even if he does not have actual notice of the registration.

The recovery of damages in the federal statute is "for any sum above the amount found as actual damages, not exceeding three times such amount." What constitutes "actual damages" under the statute? Unlike the patent and copyright statutes, the trademark statute has no guidelines such as either a liquidated damages provision or a royalty fee. The most obvious element of such damages, therefore, would have to be that of lost profits caused by the trademark infringement. But these are very difficult to prove with any degree of certainty. How can the plaintiff show that the customers who purchased from the infringer thought they were purchasing from him because of the similarity in trademarks? Besides, what if the goods are sold in an area in which the plaintiff does not compete? Has he been injured in either lost profits or business reputation in such a situation? These are difficult questions to answer and the case law on the subject does not provide the specific guidelines that one would like to portray. The statute, however, does provide for the recovery of the infringer's profits. He can do this by showing the gross receipts of the defendant and letting the defendant carry the burden of reducing this amount to a net allocation of expenses for producing the goods and by apportionment of certain amounts to those of his own efforts rather than to the trademark itself. Because the plaintiff has a property right in his trademark to protect, the fact that he is not in competition with the infringer in a given area is no reason to deny him the recovery of damages from the defendant. This is particularly true where the infringement is malicious and wilful. In such a case the infringer will be made to disgorge the profits in order to prevent his unjust enrichment. In such a situation, the plaintiff should ask for an accounting of profits from the infringer.

The federal statute provides specifically for injunctive relief and contempt enforcement of such injunctions, which are granted rather liberally in trademark and unfair competition cases because the remedy at law is usually inadequate. The issuance is still discretionary however, and the normal requirements must be met before issuance. A problem in this respect is the tendency to issue the injunctions on a "worldwide" basis rather than limiting them to the geographical area which is affected. Further, the language of the injunction must be clear so that the defendant will know what he must do with respect to the design, color, labeling or markings of his own particular product. There is no reason why the mandatory injunction cannot spell these out for him to follow.

The Lanham Act does not authorize the recovery of attorney's fees but does authorize the recovery of "costs." The Supreme Court has upheld the exclusion of attorney fees in the case of Fleischmann Distilling Corp. v. Maier Brewing Co. (386 U.S. 714). If the infringement of the unfair competition tort is malicious, punitive damages may be granted; or, if innocent, they may be denied.

d. *Misappropriation of Ideas*

The protection for a published idea is that of a copyright discussed previously. But what protection is there for the idea prior to its publication? An idea may be a property right. But, when one submits an idea to another, no promise to pay for its use may be implied, and no asserted agreement enforced, if the elements of novelty and originality are absent since the property right in an idea is based upon these two elements. Lack of novelty in an idea is fatal to any cause of action for its unlawful use.

At common law there was a property right in an unpublished work but after publication there was no copyright protection. Congress had provided copyright protection after publication on certain conditions somewhat parallel to the common law property right which the legislation specifically recognizes. Statutory copyright may be obtained for lectures, sermons, addresses before any publication of such works and ordinarily, the delivery of a speech or performance of a play is not a publication, unless it is placed in the public domain because there can be no copyright of any work in the public domain. A general publication is one which shows a dedication to the public so as to lose copyright. For example, the public exhibition of a painting without notice of copyright in a gallery the rules of which forbid copying is not a general publication. The public performance of a play is not a general publication. The public delivery of lectures on a memory system is not a general publication. The broadcast by radio of a script is not a general publication thereof. The copyright statute itself shows that oral delivery of an address is not a dedication to the public. Under the common law there were very few rules of protection for mere "ideas" and, in fact, whatever protection did exist was limited primarily to trade secrets which were based in turn upon the fiduciary duty existing between the employee and his employer. In addition, the common law did recognize what was called a "common law copyright" which protected the ideas and artistic efforts of an individual prior to its publication. For example, if an individual was writing a manuscript for publication but prior thereto someone removed it from his desk and used it, he would be liable for a violation of the "common law copyright" which imposed liability for the misappropriation of the ideas of another. Such protection still exists today to at least a certain degree as long as the idea has passed from the area of speculation and theory to some type of reality. However, one should examine sections 17 U.S.C.A. 301(a) and 17 U.S.C.A. 301(b) of the federal copyright act, effective January 1, 1978, which preempt state protection of literary property under the common law copyright and exempts certain other areas from federal preemption.

If the plaintiff was discussing random ideas on a possible book or invention but had reduced neither to any ascertainable form and the defendant took these raw ideas and used them for his own purposes, there probably would be no "common law copyright" protection afforded the plaintiff. Where protection is allowed, the remedy is that of restitution which would follow injunctive relief to prevent further publication of the document or production of the invention. Where a writing is involved, the measure of damages would be predicated upon its value which could be established by expert opinion or from an examination of market royalties issued in similar writings. In addition, the courts also look to the amount of time which the plaintiff spent in developing his idea and any personal expenses connected therewith. Punitive damages have also been awarded on the usual basis of bad faith or malice on the part of the defendant.

e. *Commercial Disparagement*

Commercial disparagement, also known as trade libel, slander of title, or business disparagement is directed primarily to the defendant's business or goods rather than to the defendant himself. Thus, it is important immediately in any given set of facts to determine whether or not the situation is concerned with commercial disparagement or defamation. The key, of course, is to examine the emphasis, i.e., is it on the product or on the person? If it is determined to be on the product, due consideration must be given to a certain leeway of expression which is allowed in our economic system. In other words, not everything said derogatorily about another's product is automatically defamatory. Today, for example, advertising on TV has moved from a time when another competitor would never be mentioned by name, to one wherein both his name and his product are compared with that of another and the statement is made quite categorically that the competitor's product does not come any where near that of the sponsor. Such comments would not be disparaging, for to be actionable, the plaintiff has to prove that the statement was false; that it was made intentionally to injure the business of the competitor, and because of this certain damages have accrued. The requirement for proving special damages is the same as is required for ordinary slander or libel per quod, i.e., actual pecuniary loss. Where the business is involved, this can be shown only by a loss of customers and a decline in sales. There was a time when the plaintiff would have to show the loss of customers by actual name; however, this has been modified by a showing of sufficient substantial customer loss by the plaintiff. The plaintiff cannot stop there, however, because he also must translate that loss of customers into loss of profits or money.

f. Trade Secrets

As indicated in the section on misappropriation of ideas, the common law did provide protection to trade secrets because of the fiduciary relationship between the parties with respect to them. It is clearly established that one who discovers and keeps secret a process of manufacture, whether a proper subject for a patent or not, has a property in it which a court of equity will protect against one who in violation of contract and breach of confidence undertakes to apply it to his own use, or to disclose it to third persons. He has not an exclusive right to it as against the public or against those who, in good faith, acquire knowledge of it. The property in a secret process is the power to make use of it to the exclusion of the world. If the world knows the process the property disappears. The principles of law governing in the consideration of such cases are (1) the inventor of a secret process has a property right in it which he may call upon a court of equity to protect against the use or disclosure of the secret by any person acquiring knowledge of it in confidence; (2) the inventor may sell the secret and all his property in it and thereby vest in the purchaser as full rights as he himself has to protection against its use or disclosure by any who have acquired knowledge of it in confidence from the inventor himself; (3) the process must be a secret process, not common to the trade, to entitle the plaintiff to protection.

While the right to do business is not in and of itself a "property" right, it is, nevertheless, a right which brings with it substantial financial value. Because of this, equity courts look upon business as being "in the nature of" a property right. Thus, equity continues to satisfy itself with respect to both jurisdiction and the application of a specific remedy by finding a property right in the given situation. It follows, therefore, that if the business itself is in the nature of a property right, then so also would be the protection of trade secrets on which the business exists. Ordinarily, the employee may well find himself in a position where he becomes privy to the inner sanctums of the business and learns the trade secrets which enables the employer to succeed over a competitor. If the employee possesses special talents, his contract of employment may well contain a negative covenant that if he ever left the employment he would not work for a competitor for a certain period of time and within a certain geographical area. As the subject of restraint of trade was discussed in Contracts, such negative covenants must be reasonable with respect to both time and space so as not to deprive the community of the valuable training or services of a particularly qualified individual. For example, they should not be "world-wide and forever." Rather, the purpose of the negative covenant should not be to restrict the employee from obtaining other employment, but rather to protect something of value to the original employer. If this does not exist, equity will not issue an injunction enforcing the negative covenant. Aside from this consideration, however, it appears to have been the majority rule for quite some time that an employee owes a duty not to disclose the trade secrets of his employer. The term "trade secrets" includes not only secret formulae, but also written customer lists and any other information which the employee received in a confidential or fiduciary relationship.

Generally, in the absence of an express contract to the contrary, solicitation of a former employer's customers, on behalf of another in competition with his former employer will not be enjoined. However, even in the absence of such an express agreement, an employer is entitled to equitable protection against the competitive use of confidential and secret information obtained as the result of the trust and confidence of previous employment. This rule does not apply to the use of customer names and addresses gathered solely from the memory of the former employee. The Restatement, Agency 2d, in section 396 provides that, "The agent is entitled to use general information concerning the method of business of the principal and the names of customers retained in his memory, if not acquired in violation of his duty as agent."

It is this secrecy of information that must be protected and if the information is no longer in that category, the employee is free to use it. By the same token, the information does not have to be covered by a patent or copyright to make it a trade secret.

If the employee does violate the relationship, whether he is under a negative covenant, or not, the use of an injunction to prevent further disclosure is proper. If the negative covenant also exists, there can either be a preliminary injunction or even a temporary restraining order to prevent the defendant from working for a competitor. If the competitor is already using the secret information, the injunction can be broad enough to cover him as well; however, it should be noted in such an instance that the secret information has now become public. If this is so, many jurisdictions hold that anyone can obtain the information and use it and thus the injunction would be inappropriate and should be dissolved.

Because of the property right inherently contained in the trade secret, the plaintiff can recover compensatory damages for the loss of his right to the exclusive use of the trade secret. The measure for this is considered to be the investment which the plaintiff put into the trade secret. This value would include such items as his fixed overhead and material costs. On the other hand, the defendant cannot deduct his overhead costs but has the burden of allocating his costs of production between those in which he used the trade secret and those of his own efforts. Where the plaintiff can prove that the defendant acted maliciously, he may be entitled to recover punitive damages; however, prejudgment interest is ordinarily denied because of the lack of a liquidated sum of money. Finally, with respect to compensatory damages, some jurisdictions will establish a reasonable royalty fee for the use of the trade secret where the damages, otherwise, would not be adequate.

The plaintiff, of course, would look to the unjust gains made by the defendant and would seek restitution to prevent his unjust enrichment. Usually, this remedy is preceded by seeking an accounting from the infringer of the profits obtained from the use of the trade secret. Equity could then impose a constructive trust on those profits placing the burden on the defendant to allocate or apportion costs so as to separate those profits which were due to the use of the trade secret from those which were the result of his own efforts. If the plaintiff chooses the restitution route, he could recover in compensatory damages only those not covered by his recovery for the unjust enrichment. This is done to prevent a double recovery. Some jurisdictions allow the plaintiff to sue on a quantum meruit basis for the value of the services which the defendant received from the trade secrets. The measure of damages in such a suit would be the market value of those services.

g.   Right of Publicity

A celebrity in our society has a property right in his/her name or likeness which cannot be exploited by a defendant without the celebrity's consent. In several jurisdictions, this right (of privacy) is protected by statute prohibiting the use of the name or likeness of any living person for advertising or trade purposes without that person's consent. These statutes differ from the tort of Invasion of Right of Privacy which is concerned with simply leaving a person alone. Where the commercialization, without consent, does occur, the plaintiff can seek an injunction on the grounds of multiplicity of suits to prevent any further use of the name or likeness. Compensatory damages are also authorized on the basis of a diversion of trade, i.e., money properly due the plaintiff is being diverted improperly to the defendant. Punitive damages may also be awarded where the publication is done with the full knowledge of the plaintiff.

Courts have held that the right to exploit one's name or likeness is a personal one and should be exercised in the lifetime of that person. Earlier cases supported the theory that the right did survive the death of the celebrity (Lugosi, Capone, Presley), but these have since been overruled. As of this time, cases involving mimicry or impersonations have not been applied to those of commercial exploitation, although some states have legislation before them for this prohibition. In addition, in the United States, in the absence of an agreement to the contrary, painters or sculptors have no rights in the commercialization of their works of art once they have been sold.

h. *Commercial Bribery*

Commercial bribery differs from trade secret violations because ordinarily in the latter situation the employee is induced by the tortfeasor to leave the employ of his employer and disclose secrets to the new employer-competitor. Commercial bribery, on the other hand, concentrates on keeping the employee in place while bribing him to do things which would be favorable to the competitor. The acceptance of the bribe by the employee constitutes the violation of the fiduciary relationship between the employee and his employer. Where this occurs, the employee would be unjustly enriched if he was allowed to keep the bribe; therefore, in the great majority of jurisdictions, the employer is entitled to recover the bribe from the employee. In addition, in most jurisdictions he would also have a cause of action for interference with the contractual relationship between himself and his employee who accepted the bribe. While this seems to amount to a double recovery, i.e., the bribe from the employee and damages in the compensatory form from the tortfeasor, the majority of courts apparently permit such recoveries. The theory of such recovery is probably that the tortfeasor has also been enriched by using the information given him by the dishonest employee and if the employer can prove such losses, there is no reason for him not to recover from the bribing competitor.

A federal statute, the Robinson-Patman Act (15 U.S.C.A. § 13(c) provides that "It shall be unlawful for any person engaged in commerce, in the course of such commerce, to pay or grant, or to receive or accept, anything of value as a commission, brokerage, or other compensation, or any allowance or discount in lieu thereof, except for services rendered in connection with the sale or purchase of goods, wares or merchandise. . . ." This has been interpreted as prohibiting commercial bribery and the case law in support of it allows treble the damages to the plaintiff.

4. PERSONAL INJURY

Where the plaintiff suffers some form of personal injury by the defendant, the recovery is usually that of compensatory damages rather than restitution because there is no unjust enrichment of the defendant. Recovery under compensatory damages usually follows that of economic and non-economic losses. The important distinction between these two types of losses is that the economic losses, if taken out to the future, must be reduced to present value; whereas, the non-economic losses, if taken out to the future, are not reduced to present value.

a. Economic Losses

Economic losses include such items as medical expenses, loss of earnings, loss of earning capacity, and loss of future earnings.

Medical expenses are those which either directly or indirectly are reasonably necessary for recovery as a result of the injury. These would include the services of a physician, hospital care, nursing care, and even psychiatric care where necessary for recovery since the object is to put the plaintiff in the position he would have been had the injury not occurred. The measure of damages for medical expenses is usually the reasonable value of the services rendered rather than their actual cost because in some cases, the victim may have his medical expenses provided at no cost to himself. If the victim has a condition for which he would have received medical treatment and that condition has been aggravated by the injury, it is the increased amount that the victim will recover by separating out the costs he would have paid for his own treatment. Some jurisdictions do not go to this length as being impracticable, so that the victim recovers the entire amount. Recovery for medical expenses is usually no problem for those incurred between the time of the injury and the trial. If the medical expenses project into the future, the plaintiff must prove, by medical testimony, the probability that such medical expenses will be incurred in the future.

With respect to earnings, the plaintiff is entitled to recover the loss of any actual wages he suffered by being away from work for the time involved between injury and judgment and to the difference in any loss of earning capacity during this same period. The term "earning capacity" stresses the plaintiff's training, education, and work-life goal such as teacher, lawyer, doctor, engineer, musician, or artist. In this context, the plaintiff must show that because of his injuries, he was deprived of obtaining available positions in those categories as applicable to him. Where the loss of earnings, or earning capacity is projected into the future because of the injuries, his recovery for these will be based upon his work-life expectancy according to tables currently in use for that purpose, which include such items as age, health, record, education, training, job experience and other relevant items. These same items are taken into consideration where the plaintiff has no record of prior earnings and future earnings capacity must, therefore, be based upon probabilities.

b. *Non-Economic Losses*

These losses include physical pain, emotional anguish, and loss of enjoyment of life. As noted earlier, when these are projected into the future, they are not reduced to present value.

The plaintiff is entitled to recover for all pain, past, present, and future, proximately caused by the injury. Several approaches have been used to solve the problem of measuring that pain from a monetary standpoint. One is to categorize the pain and suffering into both mental and physical areas and then show how each affects the victim's earning capacity, lost time, or lost profits. Another is to arbitrarily select a dollar value for the pain and suffering and then multiply that amount by the number of days involved. This is called the "Per Diem" rule. It can be attacked on the grounds that there is no evidentiary basis for the dollar amount which is selected for the pain and suffering. The real danger here is that if the injury is a permanent one, the recovery may be staggering and some courts reject it on the basis that it is only a mathematical formula. A third approach is to fix a maximum amount which the victim may recover based upon a percentage of the medical expenses involved. The major criticism here is that such a percentage may be a penalty because it may not serve to recompense the victim for his losses. This would be a particularly severe rule for the victim with a permanent injury who is entitled to future expected losses based upon his own work-life expectancy.

The victim in a personal injury case which causes grave disability or disfigurement may recover damages for the emotional distress or anxiety caused by that type of injury. In a similar vein, recovery may be had for what is called "loss of enjoyment of life" where, for example, the victim is training to be a professional musician or an artist and because of the injury suffers the loss of his/her hands to such a degree that the goal can no longer be attained. Some jurisdictions treat this as a separate form of recovery while others include it in the category of pain and suffering. Recovery for both emotional distress and loss of enjoyment of life are usually within the sound discretion of the jury.

c. *Avoidable   Consequences   and   Collateral Source Rules*

In all personal injury actions, the plaintiff is under an obligation to mitigate or minimize his damages. He does this by taking all "reasonable" steps necessary under the circumstances. Seeking prompt medical attention for injuries is such a reasonable step; whereas not doing so and thereby increasing the amount of damages to be paid by the defendant would be unreasonable and thus precluded by the Avoidable Consequences Rule.

A defendant, under the Collateral Source Rule, is not entitled to claim the benefit of payments for medical expenses or lost earnings made to the plaintiff from sources other than the defendant. For example, insurance payments made to the plaintiff from his own paid-for policy; payments by Medicare; payments from a pension fund; welfare benefits or even free services provided to the plaintiff. The collateral source rule is attacked on the grounds that it provides a double recovery for the plaintiff; however, if the plaintiff has the foresight to provide by payment of premiums for his own insurance in such situations, why should the tortfeasor-defendant be allowed to claim the benefit of this foresight by the plaintiff? Some jurisdictions do not allow recovery where the services are provided free to the plaintiff.

5. WRONGFUL DEATH AND SURVIVAL STATUTES

The personal injury situation becomes far more complicated when the victim dies as a result of his injuries. Under the common law, the cause of action against the tortfeasor died with the victim. Similarly, if the tortfeasor died before the victim, the victim's claim also disappeared. In both cases, not only did the victim lose but also his survivors because the cause of action was considered to be a personal one which could be exercised only by the victim regardless of the fact that his survivors suffered compensable damages for loss of support and consortium. To meet these particular problems, most states enacted Wrongful Death Statutes and Survival Statutes. Wrongful death actions may now be brought by survivors of the victim to recover compensation for their losses caused by the victim's death as a result of injury by the tortfeasor. The Survival Statutes keep alive the victim's own cause of action in the same manner as if he had lived, i.e., allowing him to recover damages between the time of injury and the time of death. The two statutes create certain problems. Can both actions be brought against the tortfeasor? Is there a double recovery? Would recovery by the victim before his death bar action by his dependents? To try to solve these problems, some courts insist that only the one or the other action may lie but not both. Others limit the recovery in the survival action to the time period between the injury and the death so that action by the dependents under the Wrongful Death Statute will concentrate only upon the loss of future support to which they would have been entitled had the victim not been injured. Still others say that any recovery or settlement made by the victim before his death will bar the wrongful death action. Some states hold that such a recovery does not bar the future action by the dependents because they are different parties to the suit and bring an entirely different action against the tortfeasor. Finally, some states solve the problem by having only one statute, viz., Survival, and have the victim's estate recover the net earnings which the victim would have been expected to make had he lived.

The basic measure of damages in a wrongful death action is the "loss-to-the-survivors" measure which most states follow today. Other states use what is called the "loss-to-the-estate" measure in which the expected earnings of the victim are reduced by the expected expenses the victim would have had during his life expectancy. Under the loss-to-the-survivors measure, the dependents are entitled to recover the expected financial support which the victim would have given his family had he lived. In addition, it can be expected that a provider would also have accumulated some wealth which he would leave to his family upon his death. While some courts permit the survivors to recover this loss of inheritance, the majority refuse to do so on the grounds that such damages are too speculative. Thus, recovery is predicated primarily upon the loss of the decedent's support, companionship, consortium, and where children are involved, the loss of his parental counseling and guidance. The loss of consortium finds its origin in the common law which gave the husband the right to his wife's services, including that of her exclusive sexual relationship. Where the wife is injured to such an extent that she can no longer provide such services, the husband is entitled to recover for that loss provided he can prove it to a jury. Originally at the common law and in several early jurisdictions, the wife did not have a comparable claim for the loss of consortium when the husband was injured. This was predicated upon the theory that the wife was a mere chattel or property of the husband who, alone, maintained the legal rights in the family. Today there is definitely a modern trend by statute to provide this same right to the wife. Loss of consortium, however, is not restricted to the sexual relationship. It includes all household services provided by the one to the other. Recent tables, for example, published by the Department of Transportation and the Department of Labor, price out the various services of a wife as baby-sitter, janitor, bookkeeper, accountant, counselor, nurse, cook, and many other services provided by a wife. These can be documented for the jury, leaving to it, within its discretion, the amount to be awarded for the loss of the sexual relationship.

Finally, with respect to loss of consortium, the claim is made by the one who is deprived of those services and not the victim of the injuries. In today's society, the recovery should be quite sizeable.

"Loss of companionship" is applicable particularly when the victim is an infant or young child. In such a case, some states restrict the recovery of future earnings because it is virtually impossible to tell just what type of employment the child would pursue. Therefore, they place a value on the companionship and society which the child brings to the family. The reverse is true, however, in those jurisdictions which follow the loss-to-the-estate measure. There, the life expectancy of the child and his future earnings are taken into consideration and are denied only if they are too speculative. The usual approach, however, with respect to children is to take and place a value on the child's services through his earning capacity and subtract from that the cost of rearing him. In such a case, the earning capacity extends into the child's post-majority mortality expectancy because if it was limited to the minority period only, the costs of rearing him would greatly exceed his contributions.

The least that a plaintiff can recover is nominal damages if no other damages can be established, which is rarely the case. The award of interest depends primarily upon the state statute involved. Some allow it to be added to the jury verdict by the jury itself. Others deny it completely. It would seem, however, that once the sum has been established as a liquidated one, interest should be awarded primarily as a post-judgment type for the simple reason that pre-judgment interest is not ordinarily awarded on an unliquidated sum. Medical expenses of the decedent are appropriate items of recovery in the survival action since the victim would have been able to recover these had he lived. Funeral expenses on the other hand, are recoverable in the wrongful death action. The recovery of punitive damages is generally governed by state statute although some jurisdictions have allowed recovery in the same manner as for personal injury actions. Other states have established a statutory "high" and "low" ranging from $20,000 to $100,000 as the limit on awards in wrongful death actions. But even in those states, the plaintiff can recover special damages if he is able to prove them.

As indicated above, awards in both personal injury and death cases are given in a lump sum including those for future expected losses. When such an award is made, it can be expected that the economic loss portion of the award will be rather sizeable and, therefore, be available for investment purposes. Depending upon the investment and its rate of interest or return, the economic loss award plus the interest could easily double the amount of the pecuniary losses involved. In order to compensate for this increase, the courts make such awards subject to being reduced to their present value. This is arrived at by first finding the loss period and then the average monthly or annual loss during that period. For example, if the loss period is 10 years and the economic award is $100,000, the annual expected loss would be $10,000 and the monthly expected loss would be $833.33. The purpose, therefore, is to award a sum of money which together with principal and interest will give the plaintiff $10,000 annually or $833.33 monthly. This is done by selecting a certain rate of interest, applying it to the principal, and then discounting that amount from the award to show the present value of the sums due in the future. There are discount tables which can be used for this purpose. The goal is to try to ensure that at the end of the loss period, none of the award, neither the principal nor interest, remains. If the loss period is that of life expectancy, resort should be made to statistical mortality tables in order to provide the jury with sufficient information on which it can make a reduction to present value. Another consideration with respect to the pecuniary loss award is that of inflation. Although the case law is not as clear as one might wish in this regard, it seems that the courts do consider future inflation in making the award. Awards are not taxable as income (26 U.S.C.A. § 104); however, it is error to refuse to instruct the jury that any award granted is not taxable income. Some jurisdictions (minority) hold that it is taxable because had the victim lived and earned that same money, it would have been subject to income tax. In any event, punitive damages and any interest paid are taxable.

The above discussion concentrated primarily upon those items recoverable in a Wrongful Death Action or in those jurisdictions which have a hybrid Survival Statute. The majority of jurisdictions, however, do permit both a Survival Action and a Wrongful Death Action. The Survival Action is brought by the estate and its measure of damages is the loss-to-the-estate. It seeks to recover damages between the time of injury and the time of death, whereas the Wrongful Death Action begins where the Survival Action leaves off, i.e., at the time of the decedent's death.

As a general rule, before a Survival Action can be brought, it must be proved that the decedent suffered conscious pain and suffering before he died. Depending upon the cause of death, the Survival Action could be negated. For example, in cases of death due to airplane crashes, most jurisdictions apply the presumption that death was instantaneous thus barring a Survival Action. In other situations, the decedent may be in a coma for several days, months, or even years. Is the Survival Action barred when the decedent finally dies? Most jurisdictions hold that it is not provided that the decedent could respond to pain stimuli while in the coma.

As indicated above, where the Survival Action is allowed, the recovery is limited to the period between time of injury and time of death, although this could be extensive depending upon the type of injuries suffered. The estate would be entitled to loss of actual wages and the difference in any earning capacity opportunities denied to the decedent during this period, plus his medical expenses and moneys for pain and suffering. All recoveries would be subject to the same rules discussed previously for economic and non-economic losses. Recoveries, particularly where the injuries were of a permanent nature thereby prohibiting the decedent from working throughout his work-life expectancy, would be reduced by the amount necessary for his own personal consumption during that period. The loss-to-the-estate, therefore, is considered to be what the decedent would have "saved" had he lived which amount he would have left to his family.

As a summary for either the Wrongful Death Action or the Survival Action, in computing economic losses, consideration should be given to establishing an earnings base for a period prior to the cause of the injury. Usually, one year is sufficient for this purpose and includes the decedent's wages, the difference between those wages and his earning capacity if he was not working up to that earning capacity, plus the value of supplemental benefits received from his employer. To this would be added the value of the decedent's household services by determining their cost on the open market. This would include such items as painter, repairman, plumber, and other similar functions which the decedent normally provided as services to the household.

Once the earnings base was established, an economic historical trend should be established by looking at the history of the decedent's own earnings, and then depending upon his/her work-life expectancy, project those earnings out to that time. By looking back first and then projecting it forward, a growth rate can be determined for the projected earnings over the work-life expectancy of the decedent. At the same time, the value of the household services should also be projected out but this time to the decedent's life expectancy rather than his/her work-life expectancy, to which should be added a growth rate as determined by the Consumer Price Index (CPI).

Once the life expectancy and work-life expectancy have been established, together with the future earnings as determined by the historical trend, an amount can be fixed for those earnings and medical costs, if appropriate. In hybrid Survival Actions and in Survival Actions, this amount is reduced by the portion the decedent would have consumed personally. That amount should then be reduced to present value by a statutory discount factor and in jurisdictions which permit it, inflation should then be added to that amount. In other jurisdictions, the fixed amount is not discounted to present value, thereby allowing for the inflation factor.

By using the above criteria, a sum will be determined which can compensate the deceased, so far as money can do, for the destruction of the decedent's capacity to carry on life's activities as he/she would have done had death from wrongful injury not occurred. The figure includes the destruction of the earning capacity of the deceased for such time as he/she would probably have lived but with due allowance for the effect which the ordinary vicissitudes of life might have had upon his continued enjoyment of those capacities. It is only the present worth of the pecuniary injury resulting from the wrongful death of the deceased that may be awarded to the plaintiff. It is not the equivalent of human life that is to be given, nor is punishment to be inflicted, or anger to be appeased, or sorrow to be assuaged, but only a fair and just compensation for the pecuniary injury resulting from the death of the deceased.

6. DEFAMATION AND RELATED WRONGS

The subject of defamation, i.e., libel and slander, is included in the term "dignitary invasions" or injuries which affect the individual as a person. They include such torts as assault, battery, false imprisonment, malicious prosecution, intentional infliction of mental distress, invasion of the right of privacy, and civil rights claims. The essence of the injury in such torts is to the dignity of the individual with its attendant emotional distress and embarrassment. For example, the interest which is to be protected in defamation is that of the reputation of the plaintiff. To establish such a case, the plaintiff must show the defamatory statement and that it has been communicated to a third person about him.

Under the common law, it was defamation if the plaintiff was held up to ridicule, hatred or contempt. Today it is the injury to reputation and the diminishing esteem in which the plaintiff is held. The defamation must be communicated to a third person. Telling the plaintiff alone is not defamation unless a third person has overheard it. The words must be understood in a defamatory sense by the one who hears them. If they are spoken in jest, there is no defamation. In trying to establish the defamatory meaning, the plaintiff may have to resort to extrinsic facts rather than finding the defamation in the statement itself. Those extrinsic facts are called the INDUCEMENT and the defamatory meaning based on those facts is called the INNUENDO. If the defamatory statement makes no direct reference to the plaintiff, it may be necessary to go outside of it to show that the audience actually took it to refer to the plaintiff. If this is done, it is called the COLLOQUIUM. A dead person cannot be defamed even though it causes hardship to the relatives and they cannot recover unless in their own right. Neither can a corporation in the "person" sense be defamed, e.g., by calling it unchaste or homosexual. It can be defamed by imputing financial irresponsibility to it or by attacking its credit rating.

Defamation as a general term includes those of slander (oral), slander per se, libel per quod (written) and libel per se. The key differences, which will be explained, affect the type of damages which may be recovered, i.e., special or general. Special damages are those which affect the plaintiff financially, i.e., there must be some pecuniary loss as a result of the defamation. General damages are those for hurt, humiliation, mental anguish, pain and suffering. Depending upon the type of defamation, the plaintiff may be required to plead and prove the special damages before the general damages otherwise he will be demurred out of court. As an example, if it is slander only, special damages must be pleaded and proved first. If, on the other hand, it is slander per se (on its face) the special damages need not be proven first. The following categories are considered to be slander per se: imputation of an infamous crime that the plaintiff has been convicted of or has committed; imputation of a loathsome disease, either leprosy or venereal disease, which must be a present disease and not in the past; imputation of unchastity to a woman—not to a man although there is an indication that calling a man a homosexual will bring it within this definition; anything that would affect the plaintiff in his business, trade or profession or public office. If it is libel per quod (not on its face) it is the same as plain slander and special damages must be proven before general damages will be awarded. One way of avoiding this problem is to see if the libel per quod would fit any of the categories of slander per se, usually the category affecting the plaintiff in his business, trade or profession or public office. If so, it will not be necessary to prove the special damages first. If it is libel per se (on its face) it is treated in the same way as slander per se and special damages need not be proven first. If the slander or libel pertains to a large group, there is no cause of action for its members. If it pertains only to a part of a large group, that section does not have a cause of action. If, however, it pertains to a small group (usually not above 25 persons) the statement must pertain to a substantial portion of that group to be actionable. With respect to radio and television, even though the remarks are oral and spoken, one view is that they are analogous to libel because of the potential for harm and the plaintiff need not prove special damages. Another view is that it is only oral and not written so it must be slander and the plaintiff must prove special damages.

It should be obvious from the above discussion that consideration should not be given to the remedies to be applied in cases of defamation unless and until the specific defamation is determined from the substantive standpoint. This is particularly true where the action is in ordinary slander or libel per quod in both of which special damages must be proven first or not even the cause of action will be allowed. Every effort, therefore, should be made to see if the statements can fit the categories of either slander per se or libel per se in order to eliminate the requirement of first proving special damages. There is also an added advantage to these categories—once it is established that the statements are defamatory on their face, malice in making the statements is presumed.

Where the plaintiff is required to prove the special damages first, i.e., in ordinary slander and libel per quod, he must plead and prove a pecuniary loss from an economic standpoint. For example, if the statements lowered his reputation to such an extent that he lost customers in his business or that the local chamber of commerce dismissed him from the association. Once these are shown so that the cause of action is established, the plaintiff can then recover for any other damages such as mental anguish or humiliation.

The measure of damages with respect to general damages for defamation is one which is primarily within the discretion of the jury. While the plaintiff may show that he has suffered some actual loss as a result of the defamatory statement, the injury is to his reputation which is a highly intangible thing, and depending upon that reputation, the jury may award a sizeable sum or simply nominal damages. In making its determination, the jury takes into consideration the actual statement itself. Is it vague or is it specific? What exactly is its harmful effect? Another factor would be the form which the defamatory statement takes. Is it published in a book? Is it on television or in the movies? These would give the jury an idea of the widespread extent of the defamation and its degree of permanency. A third factor is the exact reputation of the plaintiff in his community. Just what is it? In this respect, the plaintiff can bring in proof of his own reputation and by the same token, the defendant can bring in proof to show that it is bad with respect to the defamatory statement. In addition, the defendant can show that he published the statement in good faith and that he has since made a retraction of it. If nothing else, this type of action may well reduce the recovery to special damages only. Several states require such retractions where the publication has been made in good faith. Where the statements have not been made in good faith, punitive damages may also be awarded. There is one caveat here, however, which should be considered by the plaintiff. The malice which will support the award of punitive damages is that of a reckless disregard of the plaintiff's rights. In other words, it is actual malice as compared with the presumed malice which exists in both slander per se and libel per se. That "malice" goes only to the action itself and the degree of proof necessary to sustain it. There is one general remedy, however, on which most jurisdictions agree and that is that injunctions are not used to enjoin simple personal defamation. Several reasons are given not the least of which is judicial sensitivity to the First Amendment and prior restraint concerns. Another is that in personal defamation, equity has difficulty finding a "property right" since it is rather a personal right which is being protected. Perhaps the best reason is that the remedy at law is adequate. At law there would be a jury trial and once the defamation is proved the plaintiff can be compensated for all of his losses.

a. Invasions of Right of Privacy

The invasion of the right of privacy is a relatively new tort and in its simplest form it is the right to be left alone. It can take the form of intruding into the private affairs of an individual for example, through eavesdropping. Or, it can be the public disclosure of private, embarrassing facts about an individual which is offensive to the reasonable person. It can put the plaintiff in a false light in the public eye or it can be the appropriation of the plaintiff's name or likeness for the commercial benefit of the defendant. It is a personal right which does not extend to the members of the plaintiff's family regardless of the distress to the family. Unlike slander and libel per quod, the plaintiff need not prove special damages before bringing suit for the invasion of his right of privacy. Unlike defamation, the essence of the tort is the mental stress to the plaintiff rather than the injury to his reputation. Further, unlike defamation, consent is a defense rather than truth.

If the invasion of the right of privacy consists of some type or form of intrusion which is repeated, the plaintiff can obtain injunctive relief where the privacy will be threatened in the future. In addition, he can obtain damages for any past intrusion. Similarly, where the plaintiff's name or photograph are used for commercial purposes, injunctions can be issued to prevent such continued use, and damages, even restitutionary, can be recovered where the defendant has made a profit on the unauthorized use. The most difficult cases lie in the areas of either putting the plaintiff in a false light in the public eye or publishing private embarrassing facts about him which are offensive to the reasonable person. The difficulty lies in the fact that such publications involve the right to free speech and press guaranteed by the First Amendment to the Constitution. Courts of equity are reluctant to grant injunctions in such cases because of their chilling effect on the constitution. One use of the injunction in such cases would be against any tortious means to develop the information as opposed to publishing it, leaving the latter to the remedy of damages.

b. *Civil Rights Claims*

The recoveries for violations of one's civil rights are generally contained in federal civil rights statutes (42 U.S.C.A. § 1983) which provide for both compensatory and punitive damages. Local state statutes should also be consulted for other civil rights violations. Such items as refusal of service because of race, creed, or color, or an intentional interference with the voting rights of a person would be covered by such statutes. An element of damages which is generally common to such violations is the amount of emotional harm which is done to the plaintiff, particularly where the humiliation occurs in public. The motive involved in the defendant's conduct is particularly relevant in determining whether or not punitive damages should be awarded. Similarly, due consideration is given to the behavior of the plaintiff as provoking the action and may well be considered in mitigating the general and punitive damages. If the plaintiff suffers any special damages as a result, such as loss of customers in his business, he can recover for these provided he proves them with certainty and establishes the proximate cause relationship between the injury and the damages. Of course, if physical injury is involved, the plaintiff is entitled to recovery for medical expenses, loss of earning capacity, pain and suffering.

Injunctive relief has been widely used in civil rights violations. One has only to examine the daily newspapers to read of its application to the desegregation of schools and to the positive injunction for the integration of schools. In addition, it has been used to allow the plaintiff to use public accommodations which have been refused him on the basis of his race, creed or color. The major consideration involved before issuing such an injunction is the feasibility of its supervision. The best example of this has been the injunction to the schools to desegregate and integrate. Once the injunctions were issued, the courts were faced with the decision to supervise their enforcement. The result was, and still is, the submission of detailed desegregation and integration plans to the courts including the current controversy over the orders by the court to bus children from one school district to another.

7.   PERSONAL STATUS ACTIONS

The following will constitute brief positions taken by the courts of equity when they are asked to intervene in some type of personal or official relationship which is of such a nature that the court is reluctant to interfere much less issue an injunction in favor of the plaintiff.

a.   *Familial Status*

The weight of authority is against the issuance of an injunction against the interference with the relationship between husband and wife. This is due, not only to the difficulty of finding a property right, but also to the concern for foisting unwilling individuals upon each other and for other "practicability" reasons. Equity does not hesitate, however, to exercise jurisdiction over the care and control of minor children.

b. *Associational Status*

The general rule as outlined in Section 2, Chapter X, is that equity does not ordinarily intervene in the admission practices of a purely social club because it is not considered to be a property right. It will interfere if a property right is involved, e.g., death benefits for its members, or union privileges in trade unions which can be protected because they are of an economic nature. Likewise, membership in trade associations involve property rights; however, the member must exhaust his remedies within the group first. Where a member is expelled, equity can determine if the proceedings conformed to the by-laws of the organization and were conducted fairly.

c. *Academic Status*

Equity is reluctant to interfere with the administration of academic or scholastic standards. It also stays out of disputes involving the dismissal of students unless motivated by bad faith; however, it has been established that a student cannot be dismissed without being given a fair hearing at which he may be represented by legal counsel. Here again, administrative remedies within the system must be exhausted first.

d. *Religious Status*

The courts do not exercise jurisdiction over purely ecclesiastical questions, including membership; however, they do have it as to civil, contract or property rights which arise in or from a church controversy.

e. *Political Status and Rights*

Unless violations of civil rights are involved, equity will not interfere for the protection of political rights because no property right exists or because of the difficulty of supervising the relief. Besides, if an individual wants to enforce the duties of any of his officers in a political organization, the remedy of mandamus is adequate.

f. *Governmental Actions or Criminal Proceedings*

Early in equity, chancellors issued injunctions either against the prosecution of a common law action or against the enforcement of the judgment. Today, this power is limited by statute. Generally, at the common law, equity stepped in where the judgment had been obtained by fraud. Equity still has that power today but the fraud must be collateral to the cause of action so that the suit in equity is not just another attempt to get a review of the lower court decision.

g. *Foreign Judgments*

Injunctions can be issued against the enforcement of these and to enjoin parties before it from suing in a foreign court. If the judgment has already been rendered, then the injunction would be against the enforcement in the state in which the injunction is sought. If the proceedings are still before the foreign court, there is a reluctance to issue the injunction. There is a growing tendency to grant injunctions where one party is trying to obtain a more favorable decision in the foreign court or trying to make it very inconvenient for the other party.

h. *State Courts*

It is a general rule under the federal anti-injunction statute that federal district courts are prohibited from granting injunctions to stay proceedings in any state court, (28 U.S.C.A. § 2283). However, by another Act of Congress (42 U.S.C.A. § 1983), a suit may be brought in equity to redress the deprivation under color of state law of any rights, privileges, or immunities secured by the Constitution. Throughout the years, Congress itself has made certain exceptions to the anti-injunction statute such as the removal of litigation from state to federal courts; federal interpleader actions; federal jurisdiction over farm mortgages; federal habeas corpus proceedings and federal control of prices. Another exception is that of "in rem" allowing a federal court to enjoin a state court proceeding in order to protect its jurisdiction of a res over which it had

first acquired jurisdiction. There is no federal statute restricting the power of a state court from
enjoining proceedings in a federal court; however,
case law holds that state courts have no power to
enjoin the institution or prosecution of in personam
actions in federal courts.

i. *Criminal Prosecutions*

It is a basic doctrine of equity jurisprudence that
courts of equity should not act, and particularly
should not act to restrain a criminal prosecution,
when the moving party has an adequate remedy at
law and will not suffer irreparable injury if denied
equitable relief. This doctrine is reinforced by
"comity" which is a proper respect for state functions. Equity will act, however, if a statute or
ordinance is claimed to be unconstitutional and the
defendant will not be able to avail himself of his
constitutional rights in the state courts. Similarly,
attempts to enjoin the execution of a sentence for a
crime have not been successful.

j. *Administrative Proceedings*

Equity will enjoin proceedings before administrative officers and agencies. It hesitates in the area
of collecting taxes because the government may not
be able to function if the collection of taxes was
restrained in advance.

XI. REMEDIES FOR MISREPRESENTATION

1. INTRODUCTION

The tort of misrepresentation, otherwise referred to as deception, deceit, or fraud consists of those designations plus that of negligent or innocent misrepresentation. Deception or deceit is the deliberate misrepresentation of a material fact made knowingly to cause the other party to rely thereon to his detriment and damage. The main difference between deception and negligent misrepresentation is scienter, i.e, the knowledge a reasonable man would have or should have had to know that his statement would induce reliance. To be actionable, the statement must be material and intentional. If the defendant is silent and does not speak and there is no fiduciary relationship present, then he cannot be held for deception; however, there is a modern trend which is putting the defendant under a duty to speak particularly in real estate transactions to disclose material facts which are unknown to the vendee.

If the defendant says what he knows to be false, there is usually no problem with establishing scienter. In other words, the easiest situation is where the defendant is actually proved to be lying. Or, if the defendant pushes the product, not knowing whether it is true or false, the element of scienter is also present. Once these items are established, the proof shifts to see if the plaintiff actually relied upon those statements. If so, there is misrepresentation or deception. If not, there is no deception. In arriving at this conclusion, the representations can be oral or written or even by conduct. If, on the other hand, the plaintiff investigates the defendant's statements and then acts on his own findings, he cannot complain. Further, in examining the statements of the defendant, he is allowed to give his opinion or judgment as to the quality or value of an article, as long as it is his opinion. The question which is usually asked is: did the defendant, as an average, reasonable man, know or should he have known that the plaintiff would rely on what he said? If, in fact, the plaintiff did so rely, and it deals with a material fact, deception or misrepresentation is present. Otherwise, it is only negligent or innocent misrepresentation.

If the misrepresentation was intentional, and made for the purpose of deceiving the vendee and the vendee relied upon it and was deceived by it, and would not have entered into the contract but for the fact that he was so deceived by it, then a court of equity will not enforce the contract, whether it be accompanied by damage or not. Such a misrepresentation is material although not accompanied by damage. It is perfectly true that an action at law cannot be maintained for fraud unless accompanied by damage. It is also true that a court of equity will not set aside a contract obtained through fraud unless it be productive of injury. But it is not true that this applies to suits for specific performance. It is well settled that a court of equity may refuse specific performance of a contract which it would not set aside. In an action of deceit, it is true that silence as to a material fact is not necessarily, as a matter of law, equivalent to a false representation. But mere silence is quite different from concealment. If, with intent to deceive, either party to a contract of sale conceals or suppresses a material fact, which he is in good faith bound to disclose, this is evidence of and equivalent to a false representation because the concealment or suppression is in effect a misrepresentation that what is disclosed is the whole truth. The gist of the action is fraudulently producing a false impression upon the mind of the other party; and if this result is accomplished, it is unimportant whether the means of accomplishing it are words or acts of the defendant or his concealment. When the parties are in a fiduciary relationship, specific performance may be denied for misrepresentation, non-disclosure, or sharp practice. The contract will be carefully scrutinized to determine if the plaintiff has taken advantage of the relationship. Examples of such confidential relations are those between trustee and beneficiary, principal and agent, attorney and client, guardian and ward, husband and wife, parent and child, and partners. And the nature of the particular transaction may be such as to impose fiduciary duties upon the plaintiff.

a. Damages For the Tort

Where deception, fraud, or misrepresentation exists, the courts apply one of two measures of damages. The first of these is known as the "benefit-of-the-bargain" rule. Using this measure gives the plaintiff his expectation interest in the transaction. For example, if A bargains with B for the purchase of a house at a cost of $50,000 with a market value of $52,000 and after A takes possession, the ground upon which the house is situated begins to sink so that its market value reaches $45,000, A is entitled to a recovery of $7,000 from B in order to protect his expectancy interest of $2,000. The second measure is known as the "out-of-pocket" measure of damages. This gives the plaintiff the difference between what he spent and what he actually got. In the example above, A gave $50,000 for the property. He actually got property with a market value of $45,000; therefore, his out-of-pocket expenses are $5,000. It is rather obvious, that a comparison of both measures should be made to ensure that the plaintiff is compensated fully for his losses. Most jurisdictions favor the "out-of-pocket" rule over the "benefit-of-the-bargain" rule.

In addition to the recovery of general damages, the plaintiff is entitled to recover any special or consequential damages according to the rules outlined in section 3b, Chapter IV. For example, if it is a business property, he may well recover for his lost profits, if he can establish an experience factor in this regard. It is doubtful if the business is a new one. The recovery of special damages is also limited by the avoidable consequences rule previously discussed. If it is a positive application of the rule, he can recover any expenditures he made to minimize the damages. If it is a negative application of the rule, the court will reduce his recovery by the amount that he should have expended once he became aware of the deception. In addition, the plaintiff may be entitled to incidental reliance expenses which the plaintiff spends in reliance upon certain assurances made by the defendant. For example, if the property calls for the establishment of a chicken farm and the defendant agrees to provide a building for this purpose, the purchase of chickens by the plaintiff in reliance on this promise would be reimbursable as incidental reliance expenses.

What if the plaintiff is unable to prove damages under either of the two measures described above? Is he entitled to nominal damages? This is one specific area of the law of remedies in which nominal damages are not awarded without a showing of actual injury. There is a minority rule which rejects the requirement or which reads it so broadly that it might as well be eliminated.

There is no problem in awarding punitive damages under its usual requirements of bad faith, malice, oppression, wickedness, abuse and aggravation. Interest is also awarded from the time that the plaintiff became aware of the defendant's misrepresentation and began losing money as a result of it.

There is a particular situation with respect to securities in the area of the use of "inside information" and "manipulation." Under the Securities Act of 1933, one cannot use the mails with respect to securities which are not registered with the Securities Exchange Commission. If the information which is supplied to the SEC is false, the plaintiff may recover the difference between what he paid and the value of the security at the time of suit. If the prospectus itself contains false information, the remedy is that of rescission and restitution. In addition, interest and punitive damages have been authorized as well as attorney's fees under the Securities Act of 1933.

Where the act involved is that of manipulation, § 16(b) of the Securities Exchange Act of 1934 imposes liability upon corporate officers who own an interest in more than 10% of any class of stock. These persons are referred to as "insiders" who must disgorge any profit taken from the sale of the corporation's own securities within a six month period. If not, the corporation itself can sue or recover, or any stockholder can bring suit in the corporate name. Section 16(b) also imposes liability for short-swing transactions, i.e., those with less than six months between purchase and sale or sale and purchase. These remedies are primarily restitutionary in nature and the insider is not entitled to offset losses against his gains. If a stockholder brings a derivative suit, he is entitled to attorney's fees. Section 10(b) regulates deceptive devices used in the sale of securities, while § 10b–5 requires active disclosure to prospective purchasers. Where this is not done, the insider may face the remedies of disgorging his profits to prevent unjust enrichment, rescission and restitution, constructive trust, and all remedies appropriate to fraud.

b. *Contract Remedies*

Whenever the tort of fraud becomes the reason for the breach of a contract, the primary remedies are those of rescission and restitution. If the contract is still executory, the remedy would be that of rescission and restoration of whatever passed between the parties. Ordinarily, rescission is not available for an executed contract which has been breached unless the cause of that breach is fraud. In that case, the courts are not concerned with the fact that the contract has been executed. The plaintiff must notify the defendant and he must make physical tender to the defendant of whatever he received from him as outlined in § 4a of Chapter VI on Rescission. If the rescission is in equity, he does not have to make such a tender as related in § 4b of Chapter VI. In addition, in that same § 4b, there are a series of situations in which the tender is not necessary even at law. Most of those are simply common sense types of exceptions to the general rule, such as the substitution of money for property where the plaintiff has disposed of it before discovering the fraud; or where the property is fungible, i.e., belonging to a given class, such as horses or pounds of grain. Another would be where services have been involved for which money now can be substituted. A question arises where the property which the plaintiff received has depreciated in value. Must the defendant accept it in its depreciated state? He must where his fraud was intentional rather then innocent. If, however, the property is damaged rather than depreciated, the defendant must take the damaged property back on rescission, unless the damage was caused by the plaintiff while it was in his possession. Where this is the case, the plaintiff may experience a problem in getting rescission because he is unable to restore the property as it was to the defendant. If land is the subject of the agreement and it has been diminished in value because of damage to it before the fraud was discovered, this will present no problem to the plaintiff because he can offer an abatement in money for the diminished value as long as the damage was not due to the fraud of the defendant.

As far as the plaintiff is concerned, he also is entitled to get back in specie what he gave to the defendant as long as he still has it. The plaintiff can also recover the property from a third person who took it from the defendant with notice of the fraud. Also like the defendant, the plaintiff is not required to accept a money substitute particularly where land or a unique chattel is involved. If the defendant has used the property of the plaintiff and has made a profit from it or has turned the original property into a completely different product, the plaintiff is entitled to the profits or a fair rental value for the use of his property and he can also reach the new product by way of a constructive trust provided he can trace his own property onto it. If not, he would get only a money judgment for the value of his own property. If the defendant used the plaintiff's property to improve the value of his own property, the plaintiff can get an equitable lien on the defendant's property. The rule with respect to profits is different where the misrepresentation is innocent. In such a case, the plaintiff is not entitled to recover the profits made by the defendant usually as a result of his own skill and efforts. Where he is a conscious wrongdoer, the courts favor giving profits to the plaintiff even if it has a windfall effect for the plaintiff; however, where the misrepresentation is innocent, there does not seem to be any supporting reason for depriving the defendant of profits developed by his own abilities and not as a result of the misrepresentation.

If the plaintiff cannot recover his property in specie, he can seek restitution in the form of money. This can be done by rescission at law by tendering back whatever he received from the defendant. If then the defendant refuses to restore the plaintiff's item or its money value to him, the plaintiff can sue either in conversion or assumpsit or, if appropriate, bring the action in equity to have the equitable decree order the restoration. If he sues in conversion, the measure of damages will be the market value at the time and place of the conversion. If he uses assumpsit, he may be able to recover any gains made by the defendant to prevent his unjust enrichment. If the subject matter of the contract is services which have been performed by the plaintiff, he obviously does not want return services from the defendant. Rather, he wants a money judgment and the measure for such services would be their reasonable market value at the time of performance.

c. *Reformation*

There are generally two types of fraud, fraud in the inducement and fraud in the execution. In the first type (inducement) the plaintiff knows exactly what he is doing and signing; however, he has been misled or induced by some misrepresentation of the defendant to reach that stage. When this occurs, the remedy is damages or rescission. In the second type (execution) the plaintiff is misled by the defendant into believing that the agreement which he is signing actually reflects what they agreed to do when in fact it does not. When this occurs, the remedy is reformation. Reformation is an equitable remedy in which the agreement literally can be re-written to conform to the real intention of the parties. Mistake is also the basis for reformation particularly in the integration of the agreement, i.e., where the mistake is made in putting down in writing what the parties had agreed to do. In such cases, the defendant frequently complains that the only reason the plaintiff is now seeking the reformation of the agreement is because he never read it in the first place. In other words, he was negligent. This may be a valid argument provided the defendant is not using it to perpetuate his original and intentional fraud. Or the defendant may claim the protection of the Statute of Frauds, the parol evidence rule, or some clause in the agreement which amounts to a disclaimer of any fraud. These arguments are not particularly valid. If the agreement is already in writing, then reforming its terms by a further writing even though based on a prior oral agreement, would not violate the Statute. It was never intended that the Statute should be used to encourage unjust enrichment simply because the agreement was not in writing. Care should be taken, however, if the contract is still executory because the use of rescission where the parties can be restored to the status quo will also prevent unjust enrichment. By the same token, the parol evidence rule was never intended to prevent a party from showing that the writing is in fact now what the parties agreed to do. The modern trend with respect to the parol evidence rule gives a much wider latitude to the inclusion of terms where their purpose is explanatory rather than an effort to get additional terms in the agreement. If the agreement contains either a disclaimer clause, i.e., one which precludes any claim for relief for fraud or a merger clause, i.e., one which "merges" all statements into the agreement, they will not be enforced where the agreement itself was induced by fraud.

Where the fraud exists between two parties, the victim has several options. He can affirm the contract and sue for damages for the fraud. Or he can "undo" the contract through rescission and ask for restoration of what he gave the other party through restitution. Or, and this depends upon the language of the agreement as contrasted with the intent of the parties, he can "keep" the contract by having it reformed to conform to the original agreement. A problem will arise where a third person becomes involved in the situation. Assume, for example, that B fraudulently induces A to sign over certain property to him. As between A and B, this would constitute fraud in the inducement, thereby giving A the option of voiding the contract; however, A is not aware of the fraud at this time. B then passes or sells the property to C who has no knowledge of just what transpired between A and B. Is C a bona fide purchaser for value? The answer is in the affirmative but only because the fraud was in the inducement. If it had been in the execution, the instrument which passed it to C would be void and would defeat C's claim to it as a bona fide purchaser for value.

Are the rules the same if the bona fide purchaser is a creditor? In general they are provided that he is in fact, a good faith purchaser for value. But, can he be a good faith purchaser for value if all he is doing is to assert a lien, or levy an execution on the property? The answer is in the negative particularly when the victim had already imposed a constructive trust on the property because as has been noted earlier, this will give the beneficiary priority over all other creditors. There appears to be a major exception to this rule which is based upon the U.C.C. in § 2–403(1) which states "A purchaser of goods acquires all title which his transferor had or had power to transfer except that a purchaser of a limited interest acquires rights only to the extent of the interest purchased. A person with voidable title has power to transfer a good title to a good faith purchaser for value. When the goods have been delivered under a transaction of purchase the purchaser has such power even though (a) the transferor was deceived as to the identity of the purchaser, or (b) the delivery was in exchange for a check which is later dishonored, or (c) it was agreed that the transaction was to be a 'cash sale', or (d) the delivery was procured through fraud punishable as larcenous under the criminal law." It should be noted that the Code does not refer to land. In addition, the Restatement of Restitution in § 173(2)

(1937) implies that the victim of a fraud is entitled to a constructive trust upon his land over a buyer who pays for it only by satisfying a pre-existing debt. The same results do not apply to donees of the fraudulent party because they are not purchasers for value. For this reason, they cannot prevail over the constructive trust imposed by the fraud victim. Such a donee would be required to make restitution of the property unless he can plead changed position which would be so inequitable that he would not be required to effect the return. As a final note to the discussion of remedies for the breach of a contract caused by fraud, there is the problem of whether or not the plaintiff can recover damages for the tort of fraud and also full restitution? If, for example, the plaintiff wants to keep the contract and sue for damages for the fraud, can he later elect to rescind the contract and sue for restitution? The two remedies are quite inconsistent; however, if the plaintiff decides first to rescind, he can drop that suit and sue, instead for damages. Or, if he is unsuccessful in his suit for rescission, he can sue for damages because the contract is still in existence. If on the other hand, he sues for damages first, this is held to be such an affirmance of the contract that he cannot later bring an action for rescission.

XII. REMEDIES FOR MISTAKE

1. INTRODUCTION

In Chapters VI and VII, references were made to some of the basic rules concerning the use of mistake with respect to the remedies of rescission and reformation. The amplification in this particular chapter will concentrate on the application of those remedies to specific situations involving mutual mistakes, misunderstandings, unilateral mistakes which were not known to the other party, unilateral mistakes which were or should have been known by the other party, and, finally, in what particular situation relief should be granted for a unilateral mistake known only to one of the parties.

There are certain general rules with respect to mistake which are cited more or less as legal cliches. One is that the mistake must be one of fact rather than one of law. Another is that the mistake must be a mutual one rather than a unilateral one. Consistent with this, the landmark Peerless Case is cited in full support of these cliches. The subject requires greater elaboration if it is to be applied correctly. One approach is to examine the situations when a mistake could occur and deduce from these whether or not the mistake is factual, mutual, and not unilateral. The first such situation occurs when the parties are making the contract. Both believe that the subject matter of the contract exists when in fact it was destroyed without their knowledge; however, based upon their belief, the vendee does give the vendor a down payment on the purchase price. When they discover that the item no longer exists, the vendee is entitled to rescission of the contract and restitution of his down payment on the grounds of mutual mistake. A second situation may occur while the contract is being carried out. Under its terms, the vendee is required to pay a certain monthly amount to the vendor; however, he mistakenly pays more than is required each month. Here his remedy would be that of restitution to prevent the unjust enrichment of the vendor. It would certainly not be that of rescission because there is nothing wrong with the basic contract. Rather it would be more in the nature of a unilateral mistake known to the other party or at least one which should have been known as the overpayments were received. The third situation occurs when the parties terminate their negotiations and decide to reduce the terms to writing. In the drafting, the secretary mistakenly enters a different price for the items than the parties had agreed to during the negotiations. This is called a mistake in the integration of the contract, the remedy for which would be its reformation to conform to the real intent of the parties.

The above examples should emphasize that a mistake to be legally effective must be one of fact. For example, in the situation involving the subject matter which had been destroyed without the knowledge of either party, were they merely ignorant of the fact that the subject matter had already been destroyed? Or, did both believe in the fact of its existence? Were the facts in accord with their beliefs? Both parties were not ignorant of the actual condition of the subject matter because if they were, they would have assumed certain risks with respect to its existence. In other words, is there any indication that they were uncertain as to its existence? If so, they will have been said to have assumed risks concerning it. However, it is clear that both believed the subject matter did exist. In this belief, they were mistaken because their belief was not in accord with the facts. In addition, it was a mutual mistake since both believed mistakenly in the existence of the subject matter. In this context, therefore, was the Peerless Case one involving mutual mistake or mere misunderstanding? Or, were the parties ignorant of the existence of two ships by the same name? In its decision, the English court said there was no "meeting of the minds" since one person was thinking of the Peerless which would sail in December while the other was thinking of the Peerless which would sail in October. If one applies the subjective theory which the common law used in contracts, it would support the conclusion that there was no meeting of the minds; however, under the objective theory it would be difficult to come to that conclusion since both parties failed to communicate their differences to each other—hence, the misunderstanding between the parties which has been referred to frequently as a mutual mistake.

Once the mistake is established, it must be examined with respect to the application and gravity. It must be a serious one which applies to the identity or existence of the subject matter of the contract itself. If it relates only to the quantity or value of the subject matter, it is generally considered to be a mere collateral mistake which will not warrant rescission unless the parties made quantity a material part of the contract. This can be particularly sensitive in land contracts. In such, the vendee may rescind and refuse to accept the lesser amount; or he may accept the land and reduce his payments where the contract was not in gross; or, he may sue for specific performance with an abatement in the purchase price. The caveat here is to determine whether or not the acreage is tied to the purchase price. If so, the vendor is ordinarily entitled to rescission to preclude any serious overconveyance. If the transfer is in gross and the mistake is a serious one in the actual quantity of acreage, the remedy would not be rescission but reformation to reduce the acreage to the amount agreed upon by the parties.

2. APPLICATION TO SPECIFIC SITUATIONS
a. *The Remedy for Mistake in Formation—Rescission and Restitution*

As stated earlier, if both parties are mistaken as to a fact which goes to the very essence of the contract itself, the mistake is said to be a mutual one. If only one party is mistaken, the mistake is called unilateral. Now, what is the result if one of the parties makes a mistake at the time that the contract is being formed? For example, if a contractor submits a bid on a construction job which contains a mathematical error, this is usually referred to as a unilateral mistake. If the common law rule is applied to such a situation, the contractor is stuck regardless of the seriousness of the mistake upon him personally. The modern trend, however, is to balance the hardships between the parties. Look at the expectations of the promisee and balance these against the hardships on the promisor. If the expectation of the promisee is not too seriously damaged, rescission to prevent the hardships on the promisor may be granted. Another approach used by many courts is to see if the unilateral mistake was either known or should have been known to the promisee. For example, in receiving the bids, did the one in question look irresponsibly low when compared with all of the others? Shouldn't the promisee with all of his experience in the contracting business have been alerted to the fact that something was wrong with the bid? Should he be allowed from an unjust enrichment standpoint to take advantage of an obviously low bid from a promisor? Some courts have gone further than this by allowing rescission in unilateral mistake cases even though the mistake is not known and should not have been known by the other party. This is done where the parties can be put back into the status quo on the grounds that all the non-mistaken party is deprived of is an unfair bargain.

Once the mistake has been established and the agreement is to be rescinded, the parties are entitled to a return of whatever they gave each other, and this usually means "in specie." But suppose that the property cannot be returned in specie? If it is unique, such as land, the courts may even refuse to grant the rescission. On the other hand, they may impose a constructive trust upon the property to protect it over other creditors. If the subject matter of the agreement is that of services, an in specie return of services would be entirely inappropriate and the restitution would have to take the form of money. Or, if the subject matter is a chattel which the buyer is no longer in a position to return in specie, then money would be the only form of restitution left to the plaintiff.

b. The Remedy for Mistake in Integration—Reformation

Once the parties have finished their negotiations and now want to have the terms reduced to writing, it is possible primarily through draftsmen's or secretarial errors, that the writing does not reflect their true agreement. Where this occurs, the proper remedy for such a mistake is that of reformation to make the writing conform to the agreement. The caveat here is to ensure that the plaintiff is not trying to use reformation to get something into the contract which the parties had not agreed to do. It is for this reason that courts insist that only a mutual mistake will be the basis for reforming an instrument. Another area to be watched is that of the Statute of Frauds. When the parties agree orally on their terms with respect to a land sale, that agreement may be unenforceable under the Statute of Frauds. Once the deed is executed, however, the courts do not hesitate to reform it even though the original oral agreement was unenforceable under the Statute of Frauds. Some jurisdictions prefer to use rescission if the oral contract is still executory. A third area for alertness with respect to reformation is that of the parol evidence rule under which no prior or contemporaneous oral statements can be made to contradict or alter the terms of a written agreement. The modern trend with respect to the parol evidence rule is to more or less ignore it by allowing evidence of prior statements in "explanation" of existing terms so that the document can reflect accurately the true intention of the parties. The broad interpretation of "explanation" allowed by the courts has the effect of almost eliminating this exclusionary rule of evidence. Finally, one has to be alert to the presence of bona fide purchasers for value who take without notice of any mistake in the contract or deed. Where this occurs, reformation will not be granted against the BFP.

c.   *The Remedy for Mistake in Performance—Restitution*

The standard example of mistake in performance is that of the plaintiff who negligently makes overpayments to the defendant. Where this occurs, the majority rule is to allow the plaintiff a remedy of restitution to prevent unjust enrichment of the defendant. Neither the fact that the mistake is a unilateral one nor that the plaintiff has been negligent will defeat this claim. Some jurisdictions, however, allow restitution on the grounds that it is impossible in such a situation for a defendant not to know that the plaintiff is paying more than he should according to their contract or lease. At least, the defendant should have known this fact; therefore, the plaintiff is entitled to restitution.

What if the defendant orders a Ford Monarch and the plaintiff mistakenly sends him a Cadillac Seville? Is the plaintiff entitled to the restitution in specie of the Seville? The majority rule is that he is entitled to a return of the Seville which he mistakenly shipped in the performance of his contract with the defendant; otherwise, the defendant would be unjustly enriched if he is allowed to retain the Seville. Similarly, it should be quite obvious that the defendant could be held to at least knowing that the plaintiff did make a mistake.

Suppose now, that the benefits which are conferred on the defendant are due not to a mistake of fact, but rather to a mistake of law on the part of the plaintiff? Is the plaintiff entitled to restitution either in specie or money to prevent the unjust enrichment of the defendant? The majority rule is that the plaintiff cannot recover on the grounds that everyone is presumed to know the law. In this respect, it is said that the plaintiff assumes the risk of his mistake. Section 46 of the Restatement of Restitution (1939) creates several exceptions to this general rule: (1) where the mistake confers a benefit on one who is in a fiduciary relationship with the plaintiff; (2) where it confers a benefit upon an officer of the court; (3) where the mistake confers a benefit at the expense of the state; (4) where the mistake of law is that of another state rather than of the plaintiff's state; and (5) where the benefit was mistakenly conferred because of a judgment which was later reversed on appeal.

d.   *The Remedy for Mistake in Personal Injury Settlements*

In just about every personal injury case of any consequence, the defendant's insurance company tries to obtain a signed release of all claims for the victim. The problem of mistake arises when the victim believes that his injuries are only minor and does settle for a nominal sum. If the injury then becomes more serious, the victim then wants his release set aside because of mistake. In arriving at their determination, the courts apply the rules of both mistake and contract law. For example, the mistake must be a serious one which goes to the essence or the nature of the contract itself. In other words, it must pertain directly to the identity of the subject matter, rather than to the amount or degree of seriousness of the injury. For example, if A believes that as the result of a rear-ending his aching head is merely a headache and accepts a nominal amount from the insurance adjuster and signs the release, only to find that he has a serious concussion or even a hairline fracture of the skull, does his mistake go to the identity of the subject matter of the release or to its amount or degree of seriousness? Should the release be set aside because the victim made a mistake about the future course of the injury? The answer is in the negative unless his mistake concerned the original injury. For example, if he merely thought that his injury was the headache and it was the "subject matter"

of his release, whereas in fact he had a hairline
fracture of the skull, it could be concluded rather
safely that the victim's mistake concerned the nature or identity of the subject matter itself rather
than the seriousness of future consequences. Without this, the victim may well be held to having
assumed the risk of the mistake for his unknown
injuries when he signed the release. Also, there is
a consideration of unconscionability which may enter into the signing of the release. If, for example,
the victim is asked to sign and does sign, while still
in a daze or state of shock as a result of the
accident, the courts may hold that the act of the
adjuster in procuring the signature at that time was
unconscionable. Or, if the victim is illiterate when
compared with the education of the adjuster, so that
the victim did not know what he was actually signing and the adjuster knew this, there could be the
possibility of fraud in the inducement. Consideration should also be given as to whether or not the
victim was coerced into signing the release or
signed it as the result of undue influence by one in
a position of confidentiality with him.

e. The Remedy for Mistakes in Gift Transactions

The usual rule with respect to a donor is that he
gives his gift without expecting any payment in
return. As such, he is called a "volunteer" and is
not entitled to restitution. By the same token,
neither is one who forces value upon another
against his will, such as sending something through
the mails to another with the requirement that if
the recipient does not return it within a stipulated

period of time, he will be held to have purchased it. But what if the gift is given on a mistake of fact? Suppose A mistakenly pays C in the belief that he is discharging a debt between B and C and in doing so intends to make the payment as a gift to B? When he finds out that in fact no debt existed between B and C, is he entitled to recover the payment to C in restitution? The usual approach is that of considering just how serious the mistake really is. Does it go to the essence of the contract itself? If so, restitution is the proper remedy. If, on the other hand, the conferring of the benefit is not intended as a gift, but rather in expectation of payment, he will be entitled to restitution unless he is an intermeddler who has tried to force his benefits upon another.

f. Use of Mistake as a Defense to Specific Performance

If mutual mistake is a sufficient reason to reform or rescind a contract it may also be used to bar specific performance. Before granting a decree in specific performance, the court should be satisfied not only of the existence of a valid contract, free from fraud and enforceable in law, but also of its fairness and harmony with equity and good conscience. However strong, clear and emphatic the language of the contract, however plain the right at law, if a specific performance would, for any reason, cause a harsh result, inequitable or contrary to good conscience, the court should refuse such a decree and leave the parties to their remedies at law. In an equity proceeding the complainant must do equity and can obtain only equity. The mere mistake of one party, however great, will not excuse him from making full compensation. When, however, application is made to the court not to determine and enforce legal rights but to do equity between the parties, the court will be careful to do only equity and will not aid one party to take advantage of the mistake of the other party.

If the contract is obtained by the suppression of material facts known to the party seeking performance, and unknown to the defendant; or if the defendant was led into making it by surprise without fault on his part, though not misled by positive representations of the other party; or if it is impressed with any inequitable feature, the court will refuse to enforce the contract.

XIII. REMEDIES FOR DURESS, UNDUE INFLUENCE AND RELATED WRONGS

1. INTRODUCTION

The subjects of duress, undue influence, breach of a fiduciary relationship and unconscionability, have been receiving greater emphasis today because of their economic importance. In the case of a fiduciary, for example, he is in the position of absolutely disclosing all information in his possession to his beneficiary. These involve relationships such as lawyer-client, doctor-patient, broker-client, trustee-beneficiary, and many others in which the element of economic confidentiality must be protected. Just about all of the relationships, therefore, involve some form of agreement or contract between the parties and raise questions involving duress in the sense of coercion or undue influence by one in a dominant position over one in a subordinate position, and finally unconscionability where the degree of advantage taken is offensive to one's conscience. These are discussed in the following sections.

2. DURESS

Duress is the use of some form of wrongful coercion by one person upon another to obtain a material benefit usually in the form of money or property. If it is used in the economic sphere, it is called "economic duress" or "economic compulsion." The key to understanding duress is to recognize that it puts the victim in the position of acting against his own free will. Unlike fraud in which the victim is not aware that he has been induced by the misrepresentation of some material fact to sign an agreement, in duress the victim knows all of the facts but is coerced into a course of action which he would otherwise not follow. Under the common law, the duress had to involve the use of some type of physical force or at least the substantial threat of it. That is not required today and the plaintiff can show duress by showing some wrongful act of the defendant which placed the plaintiff in a position in which his freedom of choice was denied. A distinction must be made at the outset, however, between the normal, aggressive, hard-bargaining which is done in the business world as opposed to coercion in which the plaintiff ends up with a decision wrongfully imposed upon him. The fact that he adheres to his price or even rejects certain competitors does not amount to the wrongfulness necessary to constitute duress. It would have to reach the point where he actually places others in the position of having no choice but to comply with his demands. Duress, therefore, in and of itself, is not a tort; however, it is usually found with another tort. For example, if A falsely imprisons B in a room until he signs the agreement, the tort is that of false imprisonment while the defense to enforcing the contract is that of duress. In such an instance, it can be seen that the duress was to the person directly. It can also involve the property of the victim which is seized and held to extort a larger price from him for its return. The duress can take the form of a threat to bring a criminal prosecution against the victim provided the threat is not in the public interest but rather in the private interest of the defendant. The threat of bringing a civil suit, however, is not considered to be duress for the simple reason that one is free to bring a civil suit against another. If, however, the threat is accompanied by a wrongful act such as abuse of process, duress would be established.

It should be noted at this time that much of the emphasis in determining whether or not duress exists seems to be in the field of tort since it usually involves some type of wrongful act. What is the result if the defendant threatens to breach his contract unless something else is done? The majority rule is that such threats do not constitute duress. One of the major reasons for this rule lies in the fact that the defendant usually has a pre-existing duty to perform under the contract and that even though the plaintiff should consent to conditions to avoid the breach, the defendant can be held to his pre-existing duty unless the new agreement was considered as a modification of the old one or a mutual rescission of the old coupled with the establishment of a new one. It should be recalled, however, that the threat to interfere with another's contractual relationship is a tort.

The primary remedy for duress is that of restitution. If a contract is involved it can be avoided because of the duress. By the same token, it can be used as a defense where one is sued on a contract which developed as a result of duress. Resort for remedy should also be had to the specific cause of action where duress is involved. For example, if the action is that of abuse of process whereby the defendant would try to obtain the property of the plaintiff before trial through duress, the remedy would be that of the tort of abuse of process, and all transactions as a result thereof would be voided. Concurrently, if the plaintiff, gave the defendant anything as a result of the duress, he would recover it under the remedy of restitution.

3. UNDUE INFLUENCE

Influence is said to exist when in a relationship between two parties, one is in a dominant position while the other is in a subordinate one having full faith and confidence in the judgment or advice of the dominating party. That influence becomes "undue" when the dominating party takes advantage of his position to influence the other into making decisions which are actually and clearly against the best interests of the subordinate party. Thus, the prime factor involved in undue influence is the confidential relationship between the parties. It has even been held that where such confidentiality exists, there will be a presumption of undue influence in favor of the subordinate or dependent party. In such a case, the burden is on the dominant party to show that the undue influence did not exist. This may be shown by proving that the subordinate party actually received independent advice and acted on it rather than that of the dominating party. This would be particularly important in testamentary situations where the attorney who helped to prepare the will was also its beneficiary. Here in addition to the confidential relationship, the courts will accept other motivation on the part of the testator for making the bequest. They will also examine the size of the gift in relation to the rest of the estate and finally, the mental competency of the testator. If, in fact, the testator was mentally incompetent and this was known to the attorney, he may even be guilty of fraud in addition to undue influence. The stringency in these situations is the result of the importance which the courts attach to the fiduciary relationship between the parties, which requires the fiduciary to disclose all material facts to the other party. This fiduciary obligation stems from equity's idea of the conscience required to act for the benefit of another and to avoid any profit made at the expense of the other. Examples of fiduciaries are lawyers, partners, agents, trustees, executors, or corporate officers. These people are in a position where they can abuse the confidence of their principals or clients. They can do this in usually one of two ways. The first is by not disclosing all material facts in a given situation, or by using inside information belonging to the beneficiary for their own benefit and profit. Where this occurs, the courts will not permit the fiduciary to keep such gains. If the breach of the fiduciary relationship amounts to fraud, the victim can claim damages in tort. Or, he can seek restitutionary relief where unjust enrichment would otherwise result and if a contractual situation results from the fiduciary's breach, the victim can assert the breach of the fiduciary relationship as a defense. The equitable remedy of constructive trust is available particularly where the defendant has made profits from the breach and it is said that the fiduciary actually holds such profits as a trustee for the beneficiary. One should be careful, however, not to confuse the ordinary fraud case with that of breach of a fiduciary relationship. For example, in the ordinary fraud situation, no fiduciary relationship exists and the imposition of a constructive trust upon any profits made does not serve to create a fiduciary relationship between the fraudfeasor and his victim. As such, therefore, the fraudfeasor is liable for the profits but he has no duty of investing them to the maximum for the benefit of the beneficiary as a fiduciary must do. One of the best examples of this type of relationship is that of broker/client. The general rule is that a broker is a fiduciary who cannot make any profit from a transaction unless it has been fully disclosed and approved by the client. For example, the broker is liable for restitution if he misrepresents the minimum sale price to a buyer and pockets the difference when he sells at a higher figure. The usual remedy in this case is to force the broker to disgorge his gains on the unjust enrichment principle using constructive trust particularly where land is involved.

Thus, undue influence differs from fraud which is based on positively deceiving the victim. It also differs from duress which occurs when the victim is coerced by threats or wrongful acts to do something against his own free will. Like duress, undue influence is not a tort. Where it exists, it can be used as a basis of rescission and restitution. Or, it may be used as a defense in the same manner as duress on a contractual situation which had been induced by undue influence. The equitable remedies of constructive trust, equitable lien and accounting are also available to the victim provided he can comply with their requirements, particularly that of tracing.

4.   UNCONSCIONABILITY

Unconscionability is clearly a remedy in equity which developed as we have seen because of the actions occurring at law which "affected the very conscience of reasonable and fair persons." It applied primarily to contracts with equity either granting or refusing to grant specific performance depending upon the existence of unconscionability. It is in the U.C.C. today (§ 2–302) primarily as a defense whereby the "court may refuse to enforce the contract, or it may enforce the remainder of the contract without the unconscionable clause, or it may so limit the application of any unconscionable clause as to avoid any unconscionable results." Examining these actions, one can see quite readily, that damages are not a form of relief where unconscionability is involved. Rather, the unconscionable party stands to lose his expectancy under the contract. If the victim has already paid an unconscionable sum, he may be allowed restitution for all that is beyond the conscionable limit he should have paid. Or, under the Code, the agreement could be reformed to strike or limit the unconscionable clauses.

Just what is unconscionability? Where would one find it? Look first at the relationship between the parties. Is there an extreme disparity in the bargaining relationship? Does the vendor have to lift the vendee's wrist so that the vendee can place his "X" in the right section of the adhesion contract? Or, look to the contracts themselves. Are they so tuna-packed with fine-print clauses that the average person could not possibly understand them even if he took the time to read them? Are the terms so harsh that they amount to oppression? What about the price of the item? Is it so excessive as to offend conscience? These are just some of the questions which may be asked by the court in making its determination of unconscionability. And one should not overlook the language of § 2–302 of the U.C.C. which provides that unconscionability is found "as a matter of law," i.e., meaning by the judge and not by a jury. The U.C.C. in § 2–302 states "Unconscionable Contract or Clause. (1) If the court as a matter of law finds the contract or any clause of the contract to have been unconscionable at the time it was made the court may refuse to enforce the contract, or it may enforce the remainder of the contract without the unconscionable clause, or it may so limit the application of any unconscionable clause as to avoid any unconscionable result. (2) When it is claimed or appears to the court that the contract or any clause thereof may be unconscionable the parties shall be afforded a reasonable opportunity to present evidence as to its commercial setting, purpose and effect to aid the court in making the determination."

5. HARDSHIP

Can a court of equity refuse specific performance upon the sole objection of hardship where the contract in its inception was fairly and justly made, and the hardship is the result of miscalculation, or is caused by subsequent events or a change of circumstances, and the party seeking performance is wholly without fault? The element of risk enters more or less into every contract and the obligation to perform it cannot be allowed to depend upon the question whether it has proved to be advantageous or disadvantageous. It would be a travesty upon justice and the reputed sanctity of contracts would be of little avail, if parties could refuse the performance of contracts having some years to run, which were fairly entered into and believed to be just and equal when made, merely because the contingencies, whose possibility might have been foreseen had turned out, in the course of execution, to be a losing instead of a profitable bargain. The Restatement of Contracts (1932) in § 367 states that "Specific enforcement of a contract may be refused if . . . (b) its enforcement will cause unreasonable or disproportionate hardship or loss to the defendant or to third persons, or (c) it was induced by some sharp practice, misrepresentation, or mistake."

XIV. REMEDIES FOR BREACH OF CONTRACT

1. INTRODUCTION

The basic rules governing both damages and specific performance as the prime remedies for breach of contract are contained in Chapters IV and VI respectively of this book. At this point, and prior to discussing specific applications of those remedies, the subject is important enough to provide a brief summary or recap of those particular rules.

The standard rule of recovery for breach of contract is to put the plaintiff in the position he would have been in had the contract not been breached. Indeed, it can be said that this is a refinement of the general rule of remedies which is to put the victim in the position he would have been in had either the tort or breach of contract not occurred. The peculiarity with respect to contracts, however, is that such a rule will give the victim his "expectancy", "expectation interest," or "benefit of the bargain", as the result is variously called. For example, if A contracts with B to purchase a home for $50,000 and on the date of performance the market value of the property is $52,000, A's expectancy is $2,000. If B should breach the contract at that time, A would be entitled to damages in the amount of $2,000, deferring for the time any discussion of specific performance as the prime remedy in breach of contract situations.

In addition to the expectancy, A may be entitled to special or consequential damages provided he can prove these with a reasonable amount of certainty as to their amount, that they are not too remote from the breach, and that there is a causal relationship between the breach and the damages. The overriding limitation with respect to special damages is that of the rule of foreseeability, i.e., that such damages must have been in the contemplation of the parties at the time the contract was formed (Hadley v. Baxendale). In seeking such a recovery, the plaintiff must first prove that the special damages resulted from the defendant's breach, i.e., there is a "but for" relationship between the injury and the damages. Secondly, he must prove the amount of his damages, not with mathematical certainty, but with a reasonable degree of certainty. As a result of the Hadley case, which is a limitation on the recovery of special damages, recovery for personal injury or mental anguish in breach of contract cases is precluded as not being foreseeable at the time of the making of the contract although there is a minority rule to the opposite effect.

Loss of future profits is another area which is affected by the foreseeability rule, particularly where the business is a new one without any experience factor. It should be emphasized, however, that the limiting rule of Hadley does not apply to restitutionary claims because Hadley had nothing to do with unjust enrichment of the defendant. In this respect, restitution may be used where one of the parties has partially performed and conferred a benefit upon the other before the recipient of the benefit breaches the contract. Should such occur in contracts for services, the non-breaching party may recover their value in money. Or, the reverse may be true. If payment has been made for services which are not according to the agreement, the one who has paid may sue for restitution of the moneys paid to the other party.

If one of the parties has expended moneys in reliance upon the agreement, and the other party breaches, the non-breaching party may be entitled to a recovery of his reliance expenses subject to the condition that they are not already included in the expectancy recovery. The question which usually arises in the reliance cases is whether or not the plaintiff's recovery is limited by the contract price. A suggestion has been made that if the expenses are considered to be "essential", i.e., those which the plaintiff would have spent anyhow in performing the contract, they will be included in the expectancy and he should not also recover for these as reliance expenses. Thus, the contract price would be a limit for reliance expenses which are of the essential type. These are distinguished from "incidental" expenses which are those costs incurred by the plaintiff that are not a part of the price he must pay to perform, e.g., buying chickens for a farm he has contracted to buy. He can perform the contract for the purchase of the farm without buying the chickens. Nevertheless, he does buy the chickens in reliance on the defendant completing the contract. If he does not, the incidental expenses should be recoverable as special damages and without regard to the contract price; however, care must be taken to determine the effect of the Hadley rule of fore-seeability on such damages.

In making its determination as to the award of any of the damages indicated above, the courts follow the pattern of first awarding general damages and then following these with the special or consequential damages which the courts usually do not favor, although there is a modern liberal trend developing with respect to favoring special damages. The actual measure which is used to award damages is that of "value" which will give the plaintiff the difference between the value promised and the value he gets when the contract is not retained. For example, if a vendor promises to sell land for $50,000 and on the date of performance it is worth $50,000, he has suffered no loss. The fact that it drops to $45,000 the very next day is of no consequence. If, on the other hand, it is worth $60,000 on the date of performance, he would be entitled to his expectancy of $10,000. If chattels are involved, the measure, taken from the U.C.C., is the cover or resale value of the goods. For example, if the vendee breaches, the vendor may sell the goods in the market and if he gets less than what the vendee promised to pay, he can recover the difference from the vendee. If the breach involves a contractor who does incomplete or improper work, the application of the value measure would give the owner the difference between the value of the property as it is with the improper or incomplete work and the value it would have been had the work been completed or completed properly. The owner may instead decide to finish the work himself. If so, his recovery would be based upon the actual costs of completing the job. Where the owner breaches, rather than the contractor, the latter recovers the contract price less the amount he would have spent in completing the job properly.

The least that a plaintiff can recover in a breach of contract suit is nominal damages, although the U.C.C. neither authorizes nor excludes them. Further, punitive damages are generally not awarded for breach of contract. The plaintiff, however, should be alert to the fact that many breaches of contract are also accompanied by some tortious action on the part of the defendant. If this is the situation, the plaintiff should consider electing the better remedy, for under the doctrine of election of remedies, he is never entitled to a double recovery. However, where the breach itself is a very oppressive one, done in malicious bad faith by the defendant, the plaintiff should not hesitate to ask for punitive damages even in the breach of contract suit. One caveat here is that equity hesitates to award punitive damages on the grounds that they are quasi criminal in nature and therefore, are opposed to the principles of equity.

If the contract contains a liquidated damages provision, there is a minority rule that such operates as the ceiling for recovery. The majority rule, however, seeks to determine whether or not such a clause is penal in nature and provides no alternative to the parties. For example, if the actual damages are grossly disproportionate to the liquidated damages, the enforcement of such a clause may have the effect of a penalty on the plaintiff. Secondly, to be valid, such clauses must have been inserted because at the time the contract was made it was too difficult to estimate just what the damages would be if a breach did occur. The caveat with respect to the liquidated damages rule is whether or not the language of the agreement refers to the recovery of liquidated damages as the "sole" remedy. If so, recovery in equity for specific performance will be denied because the parties have bargained otherwise.

Problems may arise where specific performance is requested where there has been partial performance and an abatement in the purchase price is requested. Originally, equity did not favor these because they were in effect remaking the contract between the parties rather than specifically enforcing the one they originally made. Equity has done so in situations where the title proved defective to an inconsiderable degree by decreeing specific performance with a ratable deduction of the purchase price by way of compensation. Where advantage is taken of a circumstance that does not admit a strict performance of the contract, if the failure is not substantial, equity will interfere. For example, if A has made 47 of his 48 installment payments and has difficulty with the last one, equity will interfere to prevent the vendor from not conveying the instrument because the vendee has failed to meet one payment. The Restatement of Contracts (1932) in § 375, states "(1) Specific enforcement will not be decreed if the plaintiff has himself committed a material breach unless refusal of the decree will effectuate an unjust penalty or forfeiture. (2) Specific enforcement may properly be decreed, in spite of a minor breach or innocent misrepresentation, involving no substantial failure of the exchange for the performance to be compelled. (3) If specific enforcement is decreed in spite of a breach by the plaintiff, the defendant has a right to compensation for such a breach. This may be given either by making a just abatement in the price or other performance to be rendered by the defendant, or by making the decree conditional on payment to the defendant of reasonable compensation in money."

2. REMEDIES FOR BREACH OF LAND CONTRACTS

Beginning with this section, the rules governing the remedies for breach of a contract will be discussed in the context of their application to various situations such as land, personal property, building contracts, and other contracts. The purpose is to promote student utility of the rules which have been discussed so that the abstract discussion may be translated into that which he may use on both his examinations and later in practice.

If the vendor breaches his contract to convey land to the vendee, the vendee is entitled under the general rule to be put in the position he would have been in had the contract been performed. In other words, he is entitled to his loss of the bargain plus any special damages which were foreseen under the limiting rule of Hadley v. Baxendale. This means that the vendee will be given the difference between the contract price of the land and its market value on the date of the breach as his general damages, because these would naturally arise as a result of the breach, and any special damages which were in the contemplation of the parties at the time the contract was formed. He also has the remedy of specific performance available if he wishes to exercise it. If it is the vendee who breaches, the vendor is entitled to the same type of recovery of general damages, i.e., the difference between the contract price and the market value on the date of the breach. In addition, he is also entitled to the same type of recovery of special damages under the Hadley rule of foreseeability. Finally, he is also entitled to specific performance of the contract.

a. *Remedies for the Vendor's Breach*

(1) Damages—Loss of Bargain

If the vendor breaches, the vendee is entitled to his loss of the bargain damages plus any special damages which he may be able to recover under the rule of Hadley v. Baxendale. His general damages are those of the difference between the contract price and the market value as of the date of the breach. That date may be extremely important. If, for example, the contract price is $50,000 and on the date of the breach the market value is $50,000, the plaintiff is entitled only to those special damages and reliance expenses which he can prove. If, however, the value on the date of the breach is $55,000, the plaintiff-vendee is entitled to recover $5,000 plus any special damages as per the rules of Hadley v.

Baxendale, plus any reliance expenses which he has not already recovered in the general damages.

(2) Defect in Title

If the cause of the breach is a defect in the title, the vendee could not possibly seek specific performance, nor would he want it, unless it can be corrected. As long as the contract for sale is executory, there is an implied agreement that the title to be furnished will be marketable, i.e., sufficiently free from all fair or reasonable doubt, so that equity can compel a purchaser to accept it in a suit for specific performance. If the court concludes that a purchaser will have difficulty marketing the property because of the doubtful title, specific performance will be refused. Therefore, his remedy is primarily restitutionary to recover any payments he has made to the vendor. Some states still apply the loss of the bargain rule in defect cases particularly where the vendor acts in bad faith as would be the situation where he knew he could not fulfill the agreement. There is the further consideration that in a contract for the sale of land, the vendor is required to furnish a warranty deed to the property. When he does this, future action is predicated upon that deed and its covenants, particularly that the vendor is lawfully seised, there are no encumbrances and he warrants the title. If the vendor is not lawfully seised and there are encumbrances, then there is an immediate breach of the contract. The warranty covenant, however, is not breached unless and until the vendee suffers actual loss, such as if he is ousted by another with better title. Where this occurs, the vendee recovers the purchase price, any expenses incurred in trying to protect his title, plus interest. There is a minority rule which permits loss of the bargain damages in such a situation.

There is also the minority rule adopted from England that a vendor of real estate who is unable to convey a good title is ordinarily liable to the purchaser only for the consideration paid and expenses incurred by the latter, with interest, and the purchaser cannot recover the value of his bargain. If the purchaser is not out of pocket, he can recover only nominal damages. But even in these jurisdictions, the vendee can recover the value of his bargain (a) where the vendor is able to convey and refuses, or puts it out of his power, to do so; (b) where the vendor has expressly contracted with reference to the completeness of the title; (c) where the vendor acts fraudulently or in bad faith; (d) in some American jurisdictions where the vendor knows that he does not have a good title when he contracts to sell the land. If the vendee also knows that the vendor does not have a good title when he agrees to buy, this exception is held inapplicable by some courts. The majority of American jurisdictions, however, allow the purchaser to recover the value of his bargain in all cases where the vendor refuses, or is unable to convey a good title.

In a related matter, what is the recovery by the vendee for delay in conveying the title? May the vendee recover damages for the delay in addition to being awarded specific performance, and if so, what is the measure of such damages? In the United

States, most of the jurisdictions that have passed on this point hold that if the vendor refuses to convey the property, the vendee is entitled to recover damages for delay in addition to receiving specific performance. The basic measure is one which should place the vendee in the position he would have been in had the contract been performed. For example, suppose the vendee had made arrangements to resell the property as of a specific date and the delay of the vendor caused him to forego that opportunity. There is authority for holding that the vendee is entitled to recover the profit that he would have realized on the re-sale, plus interest from the date on which the re-sale was to have taken place. This is in addition to specific performance. Other jurisdictions allow him merely the difference between the contract price and the fair market value of the property at the time when the conveyance should have been consummated.

(3) Acreage Deficiency—Abatement

If the contract to sell the land is in gross or by tract with metes and bounds rather than per acre, there is no breach for any acreage deficiency unless it is a significant and material one. If so, the vendee may want to consider rescission and restitution for either fraud or mistake. Where the deficiency is immaterial, the vendee may want to keep the land and bring a suit for specific performance with an abatement in the purchase price because of the partial breach. The measure of damages used in such situations is either that of restitution or the loss of the bargain. If the vendor delays in fulfilling his contract, this is also considered to be a partial breach the damages for which would be the recovery of the rental value of the property during the delay period or the recovery of any rents and profits the vendor received during that same period. This has the effect of consummating the contract as of the date due for performance and unless the vendee has already paid the purchase price when it was due, he is liable for payment of interest to the vendor on that portion of the purchase price which should have been paid during the delay period. The vendee may also claim as special damages under the appropriate foreseeability rules, damages for any loss of profits during the delay period.

It is well established as a general rule that a court of equity will, at the option of the vendee, order specific performance of a contract to convey property as far as the vendor is able to perform, with an abatement out of the purchase money for any deficiency in title, quality or quantity of the estate. The jurisdiction for this rests upon equitable estoppel in that a vendor representing and contracting to sell an estate as his own cannot afterwards be heard to say he has not the entirety. The Restatement of Contracts (1932) in § 365 provides "The fact that a part of the promised performance cannot be rendered, or is otherwise such that its specific performance would violate some of the rules stated in Sections 360–380, does not prevent the specific enforcement of the remainder, if in all other respects the requisites for specific enforcement of that remainder exist. Compensation for the partial breach that still remains may be awarded in the same proceeding, either as damages, restitution, or an abatement in price. An indemnity against threatened future harm may also be required."

There is another situation in which specific performance with an abatement in the purchase price has been allowed. This occurs in a land sale in which a wife has an interest and refuses to join with her husband in the conveyance. Some jurisdictions refuse to grant specific performance or damages in such a situation. Others look to see if the vendee is aware of the wife's interest. If so, they refuse specific performance with an abatement in the purchase price. Other jurisdictions simply allow the specific performance with an abatement for the value of the wife's interest. Finally, some jurisdictions will allow the vendee to take only the husband's interest without any abatement for the wife's interest. The reason for this is that it may be too difficult to put a value on the wife's interest and the use of abatement has the effect of pressuring her into giving up one of her own rights.

(4) Rescission and Restitution

Whenever the vendor commits a total breach, the vendee has available to him rescission and restitution according to the rules outlined in Chapter VI. If the rescission and restitution are accomplished by mutual agreement, there is no problem; however, if the vendee refuses to return what the vendor gave him, it may be necessary to seek restitution either at law or in equity. The object, of course, is to have the vendee return the land and the vendor to return the money received for it. Where this occurs, it is not unreasonable to require the vendee to pay a reasonable rental value for the use of the land while he held it and for the vendor to pay interest for the period of time in which he held the vendee's money. In other words, they would have offsetting claims.

There are two other possibilities in handling this situation. The vendor may view the breach as only partial and seek specific performance with an abatement in the purchase price. Or, if the breach is not accompanied by fraud, the vendor might decide to sue on the covenants in the contract rather than go for rescission.

A third problem arises with respect to restitution when the vendee while in possession made improvements on the land which had the effect of increasing its value. Which, therefore, does the vendor pay for when he seeks the return of his property? Is it the cost of the work and materials or the increased value of the land? The normal rule is the latter unless the vendor had made prior arrangements with the vendee to make such improvements or if it is the vendor who has breached and the vendee is seeking the restitution. In either of these situations, the vendee can recover the value of his work and materials rather than the increased value to the land.

(5) Specific Performance

The remedy of specific performance of a land contract is now almost routinely available to a purchaser on the grounds that the remedy at law is not adequate because the land in question is unique, i.e., the same piece of land cannot be obtained elsewhere. The chances of obtaining specific performance are also almost routine unless unconscionability, inequity or hardship predominate. There is one situation in which difficulty may be experienced and that is if the contract contains a liquidated damages clause. It will be denied if it is considered to be an exclusive clause rather than an alternative one; however, equity does not hesitate to interpret it as in the alternative particularly where it serves as a penalty such as the case where the actual damages are grossly disproportionate to the liquidated damages. For a detailed discussion of the nature and effects of a liquidated damages provision, see § 2b in Chapter VIII on Specific Performance.

Chapter VIII on Specific Performance discussed the primary elements necessary to obtain this particular remedy which is not limited to land sale contracts. However, when a land sale contract is involved, several other additional elements must be considered before the equity court will render a decision concerning this important remedy. Those elements are the application of the doctrine of Equitable Conversion, particularly those rules governing devolution on death, and the shifting of the risk of loss where the subject-matter of the contract has been destroyed after the agreement was made. Before discussing these items, it must be emphasized that they are applicable only to land sale contracts and should not be applied to specific performance of a contract involving unique chattels (as provided in the U.C.C.), or to a contractor who is building for the owner on his (the contractor's) property and refuses to complete the construction, nor to the reinstatement of government employees who have been wrongly terminated.

(6) Equitable Conversion

Once the parties enter into a contract for the sale of land, equity looks upon the relation between the parties in reverse, i.e., the vendor who still holds legal title, acquires an equitable interest (vendor's lien) in the purchase price (personalty), and the vendee who has legal title to his money, now acquires an equitable interest (vendee's lien) in the realty of the vendor. All of this, of course, is dependent upon a specifically enforceable contract and none of the rights will accrue if this is not the case. The doctrine of equitable conversion is founded upon the equitable maxim "Equity considers that done which ought to be done." Even if the contract is assigned by the vendor to a third party, his vendor's lien is also transferred to the assignee. Where, however, the vendor transfers the title to a bona fide purchaser for value, this will cut off the vendee's right to call for specific performance and leave him only with an action for breach of contract against the vendor.

The problem which usually arises with respect to equitable conversion concerns the death of one or the other of the parties. For example, if it is the vendor who dies testate, his personalty (right to the contract price) passes to his legatee under the will. The land descends to the devisee under the will who takes bare legal title subject to a duty to convey to the vendee. The proper party to enforce the contract, however, is the executor or administrator of the vendor's estate. In this case where the vendor dies testate, the executor receives the personalty (money) for the benefit of the legatee(s).

If it is the vendee who dies testate, his interest in the realty descends to his devisee. The duty to pay the purchase price is on the administrator or executor of the vendee's estate who is required to pay this out of the personal estate available for the payment of debts owed by the decedent. Thus, the personal estate is depleted for the benefit of those inheriting the realty. This is known as the "right of exoneration".

If the vendor dies intestate, the right to the personalty (purchase price) passes to his next of kin (heir) who also takes the bare legal title to the realty with a duty to convey to the vendee. In this case, the proper party to enforce the contract is the administrator of the vendor's estate who receives the personalty (purchase price) for the benefit of the next of kin (heir(s)).

If the vendee dies intestate, his interest in the realty descends to his heir(s). The duty to pay the purchase price is that of the administrator of the estate under the same "right of exoneration" as explained above for the vendee who dies testate.

Where both the vendor and the vendee die before the contract is specifically enforced, the devolution, as describe above, still takes place, i.e., on the side of the vendor, his legal title to his property descends to his devisee (if vendor dies testate) or to his heir (if he dies intestate), while his equitable interst in the purchase money from the state of the vendee would pass to the vendor's executor to administer it for the benefit of the legatees or heir(s). On the side of the vendee, his money, as personalty, would pass to the administrator or executor of the estate who would be required to pay the purchase price of the land out of the personal estate of the decedent. The realty interest would pass to the devisee (if vendee died testate) or heir(s) (if vendee died intestate). The administrator or executor would be required to pay the purchase price out of the personal estate for the benefit of the devisee or heir(s). The best solution in this type of situation, is to join all parties, i.e., devisees, heir(s), and administrators or executors in the same action.

A particular problem arises with respect to equitable conversion where an option is involved. It is a standard rule that an option which is exercised before either party dies, effects a conversion although the contract is never, in fact, specifically enforced. In other words, the equitable conversion in the case of an option takes place when the option is exercised and this is the majority rule. Until that time, the vendor's interest is still only in his real property and if he died, that would pass to his devisee, if testate, or heir(s) if intestate. If, thereafter, the vendee was able to exercise the option, he would pay the money back to that devisee or heir rather than to the administrator of the vendor's estate. There is a minority rule that when the option is exercised, the equitable conversion relates back to the time when the option contract was made. Under this rule, the vendor's right to the purchase price would be that of personalty and would pass to those entitled to inherit it.

There is another related problem with respect to the doctrine of equitable conversion and it deals with who carries the risk of loss in case of accidental damage to or destruction of the property. The majority rule is that it is on the vendee while the minority rule places it on the vendor until the vendee has actually taken possession. The reasoning under the minority rule is that the vendee is not the beneficial owner of the property until he does take possession. The minority rule is included in the Uniform Vendor and Purchaser Act. Under this Act, the contract may be specifically enforced by either the vendor or vendee with abatement in the purchase price as long as the destruction is not material. If it is material, the vendor, under the Act, cannot seek specific performance and the vendee is entitled to restitution of any moneys he has paid under the agreement. Then there is the "Massachusetts" rule which holds that the sales contract will no longer be binding if the buildings on the property are destroyed by fire and the value of the buildings constitutes a large part of the total value of the estate, and the terms of the agreement show that they constituted an important part of the subject matter of the contract. If the change in value of the estate is not so great, or if it appears that the buildings did not constitute so material a part of the estate to be conveyed as to result in an annulling of the contract, specific performance may be decreed with compensation for any breach of agreement.

Where the property is destroyed, the general rule is that the vendor is entitled to the proceeds of his insurance policy on that property. If the risk of loss has passed to the vendee, such as under the majority rule, he should get either an assignment of the policy from the vendor or take out his own policy; however, when the vendor does obtain the proceeds from the policy, most courts impose a constructive trust on those proceeds in favor of the vendee to prevent the vendor from getting the proceeds plus the purchase price.

In any cases affecting equitable conversion, consideration must be given to state statutes which often change the strict application of that doctrine.

b. *Remedies for Vendee's Breach*
(1) Damages—Loss of Bargain

Where the vendee breaches the contract, the vendor is entitled to the same type of recovery as if the vendor had breached, i.e., the vendor's loss of the bargain plus any special damages according to the foreseeability rule of Hadley v. Baxendale. The loss of bargain would be the difference between the market value and the contract price either on the date of the breach or on the date he regains possession of the land. It is not the date of resale. In addition, he is entitled to the expenses of negotiating a new sale as part of his special damages. If the vendee was in possession before breach, the vendor is entitled to a fair rental value during this period. He is also entitled to interest or rental value during any period of delay by the vendee in completing the contract.

Usually in contracts for the sale of land, the vendee puts down a certain sum as earnest money to protect the sale. If the vendee breaches, the majority rule is that the vendor is allowed to keep this as a form of liquidated damages. This does not mean that he also gets his actual damages in addition to the earnest money. The best approach is to sue for all of the actual damages and then offset the earnest money against the judgment.

(2) Rescission

If the breach is a material one, the vendor may want to choose rescission as his remedy rather than specific performance provided the contract is still executory. In such a case, many courts allow the vendor to keep both the land and any payments made by the vendee toward the purchase price as damages. Rescission, of course, will not be granted where the breach is not a material one which goes to the essence of the contract itself. If the contract has been executed and fraud is the cause of the breach, the appropriate remedy is that of rescission (and restitution) as indicated in Chapter XI "Remedies for Misrepresentation," otherwise damages or specific performance are the more usual remedies. There was a time when both damages and rescission were not given; however, today both can be given provided that rescission is pleaded first followed by damages. The damages recoverable by a vendee for breach of a contract caused by fraud fall in the category of compensatory damages and includes such items as consideration, cost of any improvements, all maintenance expenses, insurance, taxes, and other incidental expenses. Those recoverable by a vendor for breach of a contract caused by fraud would be, in addition to the recovery of the property itself would be the rental value of the property while it was in the possession of the vendee. Offset against the value of the property would be those items mentioned above as recoverable by the vendee.

Where the vendee has a covenant to support the vendor and he breaches it, the usual measure of damages is the reasonable value of the support or other services contracted for, or their cost of replacement. Both past and future damages may be obtained. In addition, the vendor could have a restitutionary recovery of the value of the land less the value of any services already rendered by the vendee. The vendor-grantor might want to consider rescission in such a situation in which he would be entitled to recover the land, plus the rental value during the period in which it was held by the vendee-grantee. If, during that period, the vendee-grantee received any rents or profits, some jurisdictions would allow these to be recovered at the election of the vendor. Rescission may also be allowed to the vendor-grantor against subsequent purchasers from the vendee-grantee where the covenants for support are included in the deed itself because this would put the purchasers on notice of it.

(3) Specific Performance

Where the vendor has performed by conveying the title to the vendee and the only thing remaining is for the vendee to pay the purchase price, the seller may specifically enforce the contract by seeking a decree ordering the buyer to pay the purchase price. This is particularly true in breach by the vendee of a buy-sell or marketing contract. As an exception, since only money is involved, equity may hold that the remedy at law is adequate.

(4) Restitution

Where the purchaser puts up earnest money and then breaches, the vendor is usually entitled to keep the earnest money as a form of liquidated damages. This would seem to be in essence a form of unjust enrichment because he also has the land. There is a possibility in some jurisdictions of permitting restitution to the vendee for such payments as he has made if they exceed the damages which the vendor actually has. In such situations, the vendee has the burden of proving the excess of the vendor's damages or he loses the earnest money.

3. REMEDIES FOR BREACH OF CHATTEL SALES CONTRACTS

a. Remedies for Vendor's Breach

(1) Damages

The general rule is that if the vendor of goods fails to deliver, the vendee is entitled to his loss of bargain, which is the difference between the contract price and the market price at the time and place of delivery. If the vendor sends goods which do not conform to the contract, the vendee is entitled to the difference between the value of the goods received and what they would have been if they had conformed to the contract. The U.C.C. also recognizes the loss of bargain rule but in the case of a total breach allows the vendee to recover any part payments he has made on the purchase price plus damages based on either the market price or "cover." If it is on the market price, it is the difference between the contract price and the market price when the vendee learns of the breach, rather than at the time and place of delivery. The Code also allows the vendee once he learns of the breach to wait for a reasonable time in case the vendor changes his mind and would decide to go through with the contract. It would seem, therefore, that the vendee can choose either the market price when he learns of the breach or some reasonable later date. The "cover" referred to by the Code enables the vendee to buy substitute goods on the market within a reasonable time after the breach and if the cost of those goods is higher than the contract price, he may recover the difference from the vendor. When this is done, the Code requires that the cover must be in good faith, be reasonable and be made within a reasonable time. Thus it would seem that if the substitute goods are available on the market, the vendee should purchase them and sue for the difference in price, if any. If they are not, he should sue for the contract-market price differential. With respect to the market price, if none is locally available, then the nearest one is used with appropriate adjustments for transportation. While the Code does not make any provision for damages where there is no local market, under it the vendee can recover both incidental reliance expenses and special damages which are not too remote or speculative. This, of course, raises the question of whether or not Hadley v. Baxendale's rule of foreseeability applies to the Code. Some jurisdictions, as noted earlier, have gone even further than the foreseeability rule in special damages by requiring the defendant to assume the risk of certain damages occurring in case of a breach. This was known as the tacit agreement rule. The Code specifically rejects this rule and even departs from the foreseeability rule of Hadley v. Baxendale by allowing recovery by the vendee for special damages where he had reason to know of the vendee's needs. Thus, the requirement that such damages must be foreseen at the time they made the contract is liberalized. Nominal damages can be recovered by the vendee if there is no contract-market or contract-cover differential. While the Code does not specifically provide for such damages, there is no reason to deny nominal damages where the vendor has breached the contract.

(2) Restitution

As an alternative remedy, the vendee may want the return of any moneys he paid on the purchase price. If he chooses this remedy, he must, of course, return any goods he has received from the vendor. If, in doing this, he is proceeding on the theory of rescission and restitution, he must make a tender of returning the goods to the vendor. The U.C.C. allows restitution with the recovery of incidental reliance expenses and any loss of expected profit. It should be noted that the Code does not refer to rescission and restitution, but to restitution only so that the vendee may not only get his purchase price money back, but damages as well. One way of enforcing this is for the vendee to sell the goods in the market and credit the vendor with the price he received. In such a situation, the vendor is entitled to offset any damages he has had, or if he has not had any damages, he is entitled to liquidated damages under the Code not to exceed 20% of the purchase price or $500, whichever is less.

(3) Specific Performance

The standard rule is that the vendee is not entitled to specific performance of a contract for the sale of goods because the remedy at law is adequate. If, however, the goods are unique, specific performance may be granted. Or, if both land and chattels are sold together, the entire contract may be specifically enforced. The U.C.C. seems to liberalize the traditional rule by providing that specific performance may be decreed where the goods are unique or "in other proper circumstances." One of these circumstances could be where it is not commercially feasible to cover by obtaining other goods. Whenever the vendee sues for specific performance, the vendor may assert the standard defense of laches, estoppel, or unconscionability. If the contract contains a liquidated damages clause, it is

generally held not to be a bar to specific performance.

b. *Remedies for Vendee's Breach*
(1) Damages

If the vendee breaches, the vendor has several
courses open with respect to damages. Under the
U.C.C. he can recover the difference between the
market price and the contract price on the date
performance was due plus incidental reliance expenses. If that market-contract price is not adequate, he can go for the expected profits on the
sale. He can also "cover" by reselling the goods
and getting the difference between the resale price
and the contract price. Or, he can get the purchase
price of the goods themselves. In any of these, the
vendee would be credited with any prepayments he
has made and he may also be liable for liquidated
damages not to exceed $500 or 20% of the contract
price whichever is less. It should be noted that
when the vendee breaches and the vendor sues for
the market-contract price differential, the determining date is when the vendee's performance was due.
This is contrasted with the rule that when the
vendor breaches, the vendee can recover when he
learns of the breach. If the vendor uses the "cover" approach and resells the goods privately, the
U.C.C. requires that he notifies the vendee of this,
otherwise he cannot recover any loss on the resale
from the vendee. Where the approach is to recover
for lost profits, the U.C.C. takes the position that
overhead costs should not be deducted from the lost

profits because such costs cannot be attributed to any specific contract.

(2) Specific Performance

While the U.C.C. does not authorize specific performance for the vendor, it does create the same effect by giving the vendor his recovery of the price of the goods whenever (1) the buyer has accepted the goods; (2) the risk of loss has passed to the buyer and the goods are lost or damaged; or (3) goods identified to the contract are not reasonably resaleable. It should be noted that in this third situation, the vendor still has the goods but he is allowed to recover their purchase price also. The U.C.C. does try to protect the vendee in this situation by providing that the vendor "must hold for the buyer" and if he fails to do so and resells, he must credit the vendee with any amount he receives on the resale.

(3) Restitution

Under the common law whenever the vendor sold his goods on credit and delivered them to the vendee who failed to pay, his action was not in restitution to recover the goods, but rather on the contract to recover the purchase price. The U.C.C. follows this same rule and does not authorize rescission and restitution once the delivery of the goods has been made. There is one exception to this which was recognized at the common law. This is where the vendee was guilty of fraud. When this happened, the vendor could rescind the contract and recover either the goods in specie or their money value. Under the U.C.C. if the vendee obtains goods on credit while he is in fact insolvent, the vendor can reclaim the goods but he must do so within ten days after the vendee receives the goods unless the vendee has misrepresented his solvency in writing within three months before delivery of the goods, in which case the vendor's right of restitution is indefinite. However, it is not valid against a BFP from the vendee. It should be noted that restitution is denied whenever the vendor has fully performed his contract and all that remains is the recovery of the purchase price from the vendee. It is allowed where the vendor has not fully performed.

4. REMEDIES IN BREACH OF BUILDING CONTRACTS

a. Remedies for Contractor's Breach

(1) Damages

Whenever a contractor fails to complete the job or completes it defectively, the owner can use one of two measures of damages. The first, and generally preferred, is to give the owner the cost of completing the job or repairing it. The second is to give the owner the difference between the value of the building as it actually is compared with what it should have been under the contract. The courts are divided on which measure is the better but they seem to prefer the "cost" rule unless it would be economically wasteful particularly where repair is involved. For example, if the owner wants a specific type of wiring in his building and the contractor installs a different but just as effective type, should the owner be given the costs of having the wiring replaced or should he be given the diminished value of the property? In balancing the hardships, equity would undoubtedly apply the diminished value rule since it would be unreasonable to almost tear down the house just to replace the wiring for the sake of installing a specific type.

If the contractor fails to deliver the completed building at the time called for in the contract, the owner is entitled to recover the rental value of the building in its completed state as promised during the period of the delay. Others give him interest on any moneys he has already paid on the contract for the period of the delay. Still others look to see if he is required to obtain a substitute building during this period and if so, they use the cost of the substitute as a measure of damages. In addition, if the building is for a business purpose, the owner may seek special damages in the form of lost profits subject to the foreseeability rule of Hadley v. Baxendale.

(2) Specific Performance

Equity has generally denied specific performance for building or repair contracts because of the difficulty of enforcing or supervising such a decree. There are two major exceptions to this policy. One is where the supervision of the decree would not be technically difficult for the equity court as where the specifications would be very clear and the supervision required would be minimal. The other is where the contractor is building on his own land for the owner. If the contractor in that situation should breach by refusing to finish the building, for example, the owner could not finish the building on his own by hiring another contractor because every entry on the land of the original contractor would be a trespass. In that situation, equity would order the original contractor to specifically perform the contract.

(3) Restitution

Restitution as a remedy is ordinarily not used by an owner where the contractor breaches unless he has paid the contractor in advance for the work. In such a case, the owner could seek rescission of the agreement and restitution of the moneys paid; however, if the owner intends also to have the work completed by another contractor, he must pay the original contractor the reasonable value of the work already performed by him.

b. Remedies for Owner's Breach in Building Contracts

(1) Damages

The basic rule of damages whenever the owner breaches is to give the contractor his expectancy. If he has completed the building that expectancy is the contract price. If the contractor hasn't done anything at all on the contract including the buying of materials, he is still entitled to his expectancy if the owner repudiates. In such a case he gets his profit under the contract which is arrived at by giving him the contract price less the cost of performing the contract. Further, in this situation, the contractor is entitled to any reliance expenses he had in preparation for the contract unless they are included in his gross profit. In between these two extremes is the situation where the contractor has partially completed the job when the owner breaches. He still gets his expectancy by giving him the contract price less the costs he would have had in completing the job.

Some jurisdictions refer to the rules discussed above as the Massachusetts rule, the Connecticut rule, or the New Jersey rule. Under the Massachusetts rule the contractor would get the contract price less what it would cost to finish the job. Under the Connecticut rule, he would get the profit he could have made upon the entire job plus his expenditures in part performance. Under the New Jersey rule he would set such proportion of the contract price as the cost of the work done would bear to the total cost of doing the job plus the profits he would have made on the work not done. Ordinarily, damages under these rules would be the same.

(2) Specific Performance

Where the owner breaches, specific performance by the contractor is ordinarily denied because his remedy at law is adequate, i.e., money.

(3) Restitution

Where the contractor is in wilful breach of the agreement, the courts can hold that he is not entitled to any recovery; however, where there has been substantial performance by the contractor prior to the material breach, the courts are inclined to apply other rules. The majority rule is to give the contractor the contract price less the cost of completion or the value by which the property was increased because of the contractor's partial performance. In any event, the courts insure that the contractor does not recover more than the contract price so as not to enrich him for his wilful breach. If the breach is immaterial, the contractor should sue under quantum meruit for the reasonable value of his services, less any damages for the breach. Or, if the contract is a divisible one, he can recover for all completed portions of it even though he does not comply with the entire contract.

The measure of damages for restitution where the performance has been substantial is the actual value to the owner rather than the contractor's cost of construction. One way of doing this is to value the partially completed building separately from the land itself. Another is to look to the market and see what other contractors would charge for doing the same work. A third is to see just what it would cost to complete or repair the building and use this as the measure of the value conferred upon the owner. If this measure is used, however, consideration should be given to economic waste which, if present, may cause the courts to resort to one of the other value measures.

5.   REMEDIES FOR BREACH OF EMPLOYMENT CONTRACTS

a.   Remedies for Breach by Employer

(1) Damages

The general rule whenever the employer breaches the employment contract is to give the employee all sums due at the breach and those yet due for the remainder of the contract reduced to their present value   The formula for reducing that recovery to its present worth is the same as that used in personal injury cases, i.e., life expectancy as discussed in Section 4 of Chapter X.   Under this majority rule, the Statute of Limitations begins to run from the time of the employer's breach.   There is a minority view which limits the recovery to those amounts due at the time of the trial.

The measure of recovery is based upon the contract price and is limited by the Avoidable Consequences Rule.   Under this rule, the recovery is reduced by what the employee earned or could have earned in similar employment; however, here, the burden is on the employer to prove what the employee could have earned or did earn during the period following the wrongful termination.   In this respect, money received by the employee as unemployment compensation cannot be offset as earnings and such money is protected by the Collateral Source Rule.   Also, included in the term "wages" would be all fringe benefits such as any life insurance policies or pension plans now denied to him by the wrongful termination.   Finally, he could seek any appropriate special damages subject to the rule of foreseeability.

It should be noted that some jurisdictions (California) have established a new tort of Wrongful Discharge. If the employee is discharged for a reason which violates a statute or public policy, the wrongful act is not only a breach of the employment contract but also a tort and the tort rules of damages including the right to punitive damages may be invoked.

(2) Restitution

The employee is entitled to use restitution as a remedy if he has not yet fully performed when discharged by bringing an action in quantum meruit for the value of his services. Some jurisdictions limit this recovery to the contract price; however, the majority rule allows recovery beyond that price if the value of the work does, in fact, exceed it. If the employee fully performs, however, his action is on the contract and not in quantum meruit.

(3) Specific Performance

The general rule is that the remedy of specific performance is not available to an employee who has been wrongfully discharged. One of the reasons given is that the damages remedy is adequate. Another is that the employer-employee relationship is a personal one which usually requires cooperation between the parties. If the employee has been fired wrongfully by an employer, it is perhaps better not to bring the parties back together again by a decree. There would be difficulty also in enforcing or supervising such a decree to insure that the employee is rendering a proper performance. Equity, however, does depart from this rule whenever a government employee, at any level, is wrongfully terminated. Such an employee may seek "reinstatement with all pay and allowances due" for the period of termination.

b. Remedies for Breach by Employee

(1) Damages

Whenever the employee breaches his contract of employment, the employer is entitled to recover any additional costs he may expend in getting a substitute employee. Under the Avoidable Consequences Rule, he must take diligent steps to do so following the breach by the employee. The measure of damages is the contract-market price differential for the new employee. The employer is also entitled to recover any special damages subject to the rule of foreseeability. One such item would be the costs of training the new employee.

(2) Restitution

Generally, restitution is not an available remedy to the employer where the employee breaches unless there has been an advance of payments or options to the employee who then repudiates. The employer could bring an action in assumpsit for Money Had and Received in such a situation. There is also minor support for restitution by the employer where he has trained the employee from the beginning and the employee, after receiving the training, breaches his contract with the original employer to receive a higher salary from a new employer. In such cases, restitution is allowed the original employer of the difference between what he paid the employee and what the employee is now receiving from the new employer.

(3) Specific Performance

The general rule is that equity will not order specific performance of a contract which has the effect of forcing the employee to work for a specific employer. In addition to the personal reasons involved, there is also the consideration of the Thirteenth Amendment's prohibition against involuntary servitude. This can be overcome, however, where the contract of employment contains a negative covenant whereby the employee agrees not to work for another during the period of the contract. Or, the covenant may be not to compete after the employment is terminated. In the case of the negative covenant, equity issues an injunction to enforce it usually where the employee's services are unique by ordering the employee not to work for anyone else per the negative covenant. In the second situation, equity will first examine the skills and talents of the employee to satisfy itself that either his self-employment or that with a competitor would impose a definite hardship on the former employer. Then equity will examine the restraints with respect to both time and space to make sure they are reasonable. If so, they will issue the injunction to uphold the covenant; however, if the restraints are

unreasonable, such as not allowing the former employee "to work anywhere at any time," equity will
consider them to be an unreasonable restraint on
trade and deny the injunction.   Other courts may
"blue pencil" the offensive restraints and enforce
the reasonable ones.   Still others strike the offensive restraints completely and even insert reasonable ones where the balancing of the hardships
would indicate it.

XV. RESTITUTION FOR UNENFORCEABLE CONTRACTS

1. INTRODUCTION

Up to this point in discussing remedies for breaches of contracts, the concern has been to identify what would otherwise be a valid agreement between the parties which has been breached or repudiated in such a manner as to give the injured party the right to some type of recovery. In other words, the contract would have been performed except for some positive act by one of the parties which caused it to fail. There are contracts, however, which because of the status of the parties or the subject matter itself, will end up to be unenforceable. In many of these, the courts will say that "we will leave the parties where we find them." Does this mean that where one of the parties is in fact a victim that he cannot recover anything? The answer to this question will depend upon the type of problem involved as discussed below.

2. STATUTE OF FRAUDS

If the agreement between the parties is one which is required to be in writing by the Statute of Frauds, and it is not, such an oral agreement, depending upon the jurisdiction, may be considered either as void or unenforceable. Now suppose that the plaintiff has either rendered services or paid money to the defendant under the agreement before it is discovered that it should have been in writing? Does this mean that the plaintiff will lose his money or not receive anything for the value of his services? The answer to this lies in the remedy of restitution which is designed to prevent the unjust enrichment of the defendant. Where he has paid money, he will be entitled to recover it back from the defendant. If it is services, he may get their reasonable market value, or the value by which they benefited the defendant. There is a question as to whether or not the contract price would be used particularly when the contract itself is either void or unenforceable. In applying the measure of the value of the benefits conferred upon the defendant, the contract price may be used as some evidence of that value.

There are also situations in which the plaintiff spends money on certain expenses in reliance on the contract before it is found to be unenforceable under the Statute of Frauds. Obviously, these would not confer any benefits on the defendant and he should not, therefore, be required to restore them in restitution to the plaintiff. Care should be taken, however, to insure that the defendant does not, in fact, receive any benefit from what the plaintiff has done. If, for example, the defendant has bargained with the plaintiff for the services, and the plaintiff has accrued expenses in reliance on the bargaining, the fact that the defendant has not actually received the benefit does not mean that the service he bargained for is of no value to him. Some courts, therefore, have given recovery for the reliance expenses under the guise of finding that the defendant's bargaining for the services did confer a benefit upon him. Other courts just allow the expenses without trying to find any benefit to the defendant. Consideration should be given to determining if fraud was involved in obtaining the contract which is now unenforceable because of the Statute of Frauds. If so, recovery of the reliance expenses can be made by bringing the action in tort.

It will be recalled from Contracts law that sufficient part performance will take an oral contract out of the Statute of Frauds and make it enforceable. Usually, the ideal situation is where the vendee pays the money, takes possession of the property and makes improvements on it. The use then of the defense of Statute of Frauds to defeat the contract will not avail the vendor, and he will be required to furnish the deed to the vendee. Problems develop when less than three of these actions are involved in the part performance. For example, if the vendee should take possession of the property but neither makes any payments nor provides any improvements before the Statute of Frauds renders the agreement unenforceable and the mere taking of possession is not considered to be sufficient part performance to take it out of the Statute. In such a situation can the vendor recover his land by way of restitution? The answer is in the affirmative and it is accomplished by imposing a constructive trust on the property in the vendor's favor. This, then, will give him an in specie recovery.

In addition to sufficient part performance taking the oral agreement out of the Statute of Frauds, the plaintiff may attempt to assert that the defendant is estopped from using the Statute as a defense. This may be asserted if the plaintiff can prove detrimental reliance on the promise of the defendant to convey. He does this by showing that the promise which was given was such that the promisor knew that it would evoke reliance; that, in fact, it did evoke that reliance; that because of this, the promisee has suffered economic loss and that the promisor is aware of this injury. Thus, many courts use either sufficient part performance or estoppel by way of detrimental reliance to take the oral agreement out of the Statute of Frauds and enforce it.

3. INCAPACITY

As a general rule, whenever it is determined that one of the parties is suffering from some type of incompetency or incapacity, such as a minor, insane person, or one who was intoxicated at the time of the making of the agreement, such agreements are considered to be voidable at the option of the one with the defective capacity. When he notifies the other party that he is exercising his option to rescind the agreement, he is entitled to have returned to him whatever he gave the other. In other words, rescission followed by restitution. Where a minor is involved, he is afforded extra protection. He has the right to disaffirm at any time in his minority and for a reasonable time after he attains his majority. Whenever he does exercise this right, the other party must return to the minor whatever he gave him or at least its reasonable value. The minor, on the other hand, is only required to return whatever he received from the other party provided he has not wasted or consumed it. Some jurisdictions do not follow this view and require the minor to restore either the goods to the other party or their value. The protection given the minor even extends to bona fide purchasers. If the minor sells property to another who passes it on to a third party who takes for value and without notice of the defective capacity, the minor can still obtain the restitution of his property from the BFP. This was the rule at common law and there does not appear to be any change in the language of the U.C.C.

Where the party is incompetent because of a mental defect, the courts have drawn a distinction between whether or not the defect is so serious as to require a guardian. If so, it is only the guardian who can contract for the incompetent's estate. If this is not the situation and the vendor has acted in good faith and without any knowledge of the vendee's defect, the courts will either enforce the contract or allow the incompetent to avoid it provided he can make full restitution to the vendor. If the vendor is aware of the defective capacity, the vendee can avoid the contract by returning what he received under it or at least returning what is left of it. By the same token, he is entitled to whatever he gave the vendor in exchange.

If the vendee is so intoxicated at the time he makes the agreement that he does not realize the consequences of his act, the contract will be voidable at his option when he sobers up. The probabilities of the vendor claiming that he was not aware of the vendee's condition at the time of signing the agreement, are rather minimal when compared to that of the mentally defective party who may be acting lucidly when the agreement was made. If the intoxicant decides to avoid the contract, he does so by returning whatever he received from the vendor or what is left of it and receiving from the vendor that which he gave to him.

A problem with respect to restitution may arise in ultra vires contracts with either private or municipal corporations. As a general rule in such matters, the courts hold that if the other party has performed either fully or partially, the corporation is estopped from asserting the ultra vires defense. If the corporation has general powers to act, it can be held on the theory of quasi-contract to prevent unjust enrichment and thus give the injured party a restitution. If the corporation, particularly a municipality, is limited in contracting by statute, the majority rule is to deny restitution even though there has been an unjust enrichment of the municipality. The main reason is that the courts cannot overturn the applicable statute. There is a minority rule which allows restitution where its refusal would only encourage some form of official corruption. Where restitution is given, its measure is the value of the benefit conferred upon the municipality rather than the costs of the contractor and the contract price will serve as a ceiling on his recovery. Some claimants have tried to use the estoppel theory in the form of detrimental reliance to have the contract enforced. This, of course, would be using a means of circumventing the specific statute which prohibited the contracting and because of this, neither states nor local governments are subject to this doctrine. With respect to the federal government, sovereign immunity to suit is the appropriate defense except where it has been waived by statute in which case the contractor can recover under either his express or implied-in-fact contract. The federal government, however, is not liable for restitution on the theory of quasi-contract.

4. ILLEGALITY

As should be recalled from Contracts law, if the subject matter of an agreement is illegal, the contract is void so that even restitution of any benefits conferred is denied. There are several exceptions to this rule, one of which is that the defendant can recover if the parties are not in pari delicto, i.e., one party is more guilty than the other. If they are equally at fault, neither restitution nor enforcement of the agreement will be allowed. Where they are not equally at fault and the subject matter does not involve any serious moral turpitude such as the bribing of a public official, the less guilty of the two is entitled to restitution. Another exception would be where one of the parties entered the agreement under a mistake of fact as to its illegality. In such a situation, the contract could either be enforced or at least restitution be allowed to the mistaken party. If the mistake is one of law, however, his ignorance will not be accepted unless the ignorance was induced by the other party's misconduct. A third exception would apply where the contract is divisible, i.e., the illegal part can be separated from the legal part. Where this can be done without any reference to the illegal part, the plaintiff is entitled to have the legal part enforced. A fourth exception would be if after making the illegal agreement, but before it is carried into execution, one of the parties steps out of it. This, under Contracts law, is known as the doctrine of locus poenitentiae and it will apply unless the subject matter is that of serious moral turpitude. A fifth exception obtains where there is a fiduciary relationship and the fiduciary is withholding the property because of the illegality of the subject matter. Restitution is generally allowed not only because of the unjust enrichment but because of the breach of the fiduciary relationship. Finally, even though the parties are in pari delicto, the plaintiff should be allowed to recover where the agreement violates the federal anti-trust laws.

INDEX

References are to Pages

[307]

INDEX

INDEX

References are to Pages

INDEX

References are to Pages

INDEX

References are to Pages

INDEX

INDEX

References are to Pages

†